T0311741

Cambridge Elements ≡

Elements in Economics of European Integration
edited by
Nauro F. Campos
University College London

COMPLETING A GENUINE ECONOMIC AND MONETARY UNION

Iain Begg
*The London School of Economics
and Political Science*

CAMBRIDGE
UNIVERSITY PRESS

Shaftesbury Road, Cambridge CB2 8EA, United Kingdom

One Liberty Plaza, 20th Floor, New York, NY 10006, USA

477 Williamstown Road, Port Melbourne, VIC 3207, Australia

314–321, 3rd Floor, Plot 3, Splendor Forum, Jasola District Centre, New Delhi – 110025, India

103 Penang Road, #05–06/07, Visioncrest Commercial, Singapore 238467

Cambridge University Press is part of Cambridge University Press & Assessment, a department of the University of Cambridge.

We share the University's mission to contribute to society through the pursuit of education, learning and research at the highest international levels of excellence.

www.cambridge.org
Information on this title: www.cambridge.org/9781108965552

DOI: 10.1017/9781108963503

First published 2023

A catalogue record for this publication is available from the British Library.

ISBN 978-1-108-96555-2 Paperback
ISSN 2634-0763 (online)
ISSN 2634-0755 (print)

Completing a Genuine Economic and Monetary Union

Elements in Economics of European Integration

DOI: 10.1017/9781108963503
First published online: January 2023

Iain Begg
The London School of Economics and Political Science

Author for correspondence: Iain Begg, IAIN.Begg@lse.ac.uk

Abstract: This Element examines efforts to strengthen economic and monetary union (EMU) in the European Union (EU), especially over the last decade, asking if enough has been done to render it more sustainable and resilient. Drawing on a survey of 111 leading experts on the economics and politics of EMU, this Element reviews the wide-ranging reforms undertaken since the crises of the early 2010s and assesses whether they go far enough. Although it concludes that much has been done to push the euro towards being a more complete currency, it identifies remaining flaws and challenges that EU leaders need to resolve.

Keywords: future of EMU, governance of the Eurozone, Eurozone crises, fiscal union in Europe, banking union in Europe

ISBNs: 9781108965552 (PB), 9781108963503 (OC)
ISSNs: 2634-0763 (online), 2634-0755 (print)

Contents

1 Introduction

The creation of the euro was, by any reasonable standard, a bold extension of the European integration project. From the ruins of World War II, Europe's leaders had moved by stages from the limited industrial cooperation of the European Coal and Steel Community, established in 1951, to the single European market, with its four freedoms of movement of goods, services, labour and capital. By the early 1990s, this market integration was – though still subject to many sources of friction and tension – well on its way to completion.

Plans for monetary integration in Europe had been under consideration from the 1960s, but only came to fruition right at the end of the twentieth century (De Grauwe, 2022; Pomfret, 2021). This long gestation can be explained in a number of ways. Proposals for a monetary union elaborated in the 1970s fell foul of a succession of economic crises after the so-called *trentes glorieuses*, the long period of post-war growth up to 1973. Disagreements about how to construct a monetary union were legion and compromises hard to find (McNamara, 1998; Dyson and Featherstone, 1999). More fundamentally, two widely recognised defining attributes of a state have long been security and the currency; forgoing the latter, especially for the likes of Germany, where a strong and stable Deutsche Mark (DM) had so much symbolic value, was always going to be politically challenging.

Economic and monetary union (EMU) is a wide-ranging project because of the adjective 'economic'. A monetary union on its own would mean integration only of the currency, whereas including economic in the union implies the integration of a variety of other policies. Today, EMU in Europe has to be understood in this broader sense as many of the difficulties and challenges it faces are beyond the scope of monetary policy alone.

Initial attempts at monetary cooperation in the early 1970s – sometimes referred to as the 'snake-in-the-tunnel', limiting exchange rate fluctuations among European Union (EU) members, while providing flexibility for movements vis-à-vis third countries – rapidly fell apart when oil prices soared after the Yom Kippur war. The more comprehensive European Monetary System, introduced in 1979, did succeed in stabilising exchange rates, but had a variety of in-built tensions and was widely seen as a step towards monetary union, not an end in itself. The Maastricht Treaty agreed in 1990 then paved the way for the creation of the single currency.

1.1 The Euro's Ups and Downs

After its launch, the euro seemed to prosper. Monetary policy, though not without its critics and occasional challenges from governments who each felt that it should bend more to their own country's needs, functioned as intended and, as the

European Central Bank (ECB) has often stated, price stability was achieved. Notes and coins were introduced on schedule and with only mild tensions: who now remembers the derogatory term 'teuro' – a play on the German word for 'expensive' – used in Germany to capture the slight rounding-up of prices by retailers when the DM was replaced? The euro rapidly accounted for some 20 per cent of international reserves and financial markets accepted the new kid on the block. More broadly, the governance of EMU, though again not without its critics and clashes (especially over public finances), generally functioned as intended.

When the global financial crisis struck in 2007, the euro (and the Eurozone) initially seemed less affected than other major currencies, although it was then hit by what is now known as the sovereign debt crisis. The consensus now is that, in its first decade, the euro had flattered to deceive, notwithstanding the many celebrations as it reached its tenth birthday. A decade later, the storyline was very different. As others recovered from the global financial crisis, shortcomings in the design of the euro, compounded by policy errors and an inability to agree on solutions, were cruelly exposed. Many pundits were ready to write EMU's obituary when the sovereign debt crisis was at its worst in the early 2010s. These failings prompted a far-reaching and (at least by EU standards) almost frenetic effort to re-engineer the governance framework. Despite some hiccoughs, the euro survived, and few would now question its durability.

These efforts have, variously, been described as 'completing' EMU or establishing a 'genuine' EMU. The title of this Element conflates these two phrases. In 2012, blueprints emanating from the EU institutions listed a series of prerequisites for arriving at a 'deep and genuine EMU'. This was followed three years later by a somewhat less ambitious roadmap for 'completing economic and monetary union'. Both gave rise to policy initiatives and institutional developments intended to bolster the resilience and effectiveness of the governance of the euro. However, progress was slow and often contested, even before the pandemic struck, and the conjunction of rising energy prices and the war in Ukraine further postponed the enactment of many initiatives.

1.2 About This Element

This Element looks at the evolution of the euro, especially over the last decade, asking if enough has been done to render it more sustainable and resilient. These questions have acquired new salience as a result of geopolitical developments. The pandemic, the surge in inflation and the ramifications of the Russian invasion of Ukraine have called into question how the EU can work collectively, obliging Europe's leaders to review their approach to what might be called domestic-first economic policies and political preferences. It may provide incentives for more rapid and decisive innovation in the governance of EMU. On the other hand, the sheer magnitude of the current challenges may put on hold many of the reforms winding their way through the system and it is unclear how the euro will be affected.

To gauge opinion on what is likely to happen next in the evolution of the euro, a survey of experts on the euro was conducted in the second semester of 2020, specifically for this Element.[*] The approach was to pose a mix of structured and open questions focussed on some of the main areas of contestation about what is needed for the euro to prosper. The survey is not representative, but rather was a means of tapping into the expert knowledge of the range of people approached. It elicited 111 responses from nationals of 25 countries (including 3 outside Europe), achieving a response rate of around 80 per cent of those approached, with only 3 explicit refusals to participate. The biggest proportion of the respondents is academics, with the balance made up of practitioners, journalists, politicians and researchers in think tanks.

The completion rate of questions was very high, in some instances with explanatory comments substituting for tick-box answers. Where the respondents have given explicit permission to do so, certain comments are quoted verbatim and attributed. In other cases, to protect the identity of the respondent, quotes are presented anonymously.

Section 2 looks back at the debates and doubts about the wisdom of creating the single currency and examines the various views on why problems arose, then Section 3 ponders the meaning of a complete EMU. An overview of the performance of EMU is presented in Section 4, focussing on how and why problems arose. Section 5 sets out the main reforms in response to these problems, and how they sought to establish a 'genuine' EMU. In Section 6 the survey findings on how to ensure the long-term success of a complete and genuine EMU are summarised. Section 7 then looks at what remains to be done and considers the implications of recent geopolitical developments, and Section 8 concludes.

2 Was the EMU Project Wise?

Euro-scepticism is a phrase now associated with Brexit and insurgent populist parties opposed to European integration. Thirty years ago, a rather different scepticism was about whether creating the euro would be economically and – maybe less prominently – politically wise. Many in the economics profession, especially in the United States, had strong reservations about EMU's prospects, a stance summed up

---

[*] The author is immensely grateful to the respondents for taking the time to complete the survey and for the care taken in answering the questions.

in the title of an article by Jonung and Drea (2010): 'The euro: It can't happen. It's a bad idea. It won't last. US economists on the EMU, 1989–2002'.

Their survey covered 130 academic papers by economists based in the United States and 40 by authors working within the Federal Reserve System. The latter were found to be more concerned about the practicalities of assessing eligibility for acceding to the euro, but also the implications for the dollar. But they, too, were prone to scepticism, as demonstrated by the title of an article by Adam Zaretsky (1998) of the Federal Reserve Bank of Saint Louis: 'Yes, this EMU will fly, but will it stay aloft?'.

Academic economists, by contrast, 'focused on weaknesses and problems in the monetary integration process, usually in long papers involving models and econometric tests' (Jonung and Drea, 2010, p. 9). The reasoning was strongly influenced by the theory of the optimum currency area (OCA) and the analytic conclusion that, because the putative new currency area was far from being one, it would struggle. In a cost–benefit framework, the more distant a currency union is from optimality the greater will be the net costs. Martin Feldstein is said to have predicted that it would lead to war, although what he actually wrote in *Foreign Affairs* was that 'it will change the political character of Europe in ways that could lead to conflicts in Europe and confrontations with the United States'.[1]

James Tobin (2001, p. 31), writing shortly before the introduction of euro notes and coins, yet more than two years beyond the delegation of monetary policy to the ECB (at the start of 1999), refers to the launch of the single currency as 'the euro experiment' (a phrase echoed by others, such as Schelkle, 2018 and Wallace, 2016, implying an easily reversible trial) and, contrasting it with the roots of the dollar, observes that the Maastricht Treaty is not the US Constitution. He goes on to issue a stark warning: 'without far-ranging changes to European institutions, it is hard to see how the euro can succeed'. Tobin compares some key attributes of the dollar and the architecture of the (then infant) euro to underpin his warning, citing:

• the narrower focus of Eurozone monetary policy on price stability, in contrast to the Fed's dual mandate, which enables it to act to curb unemployment;
• the lack of fiscal capacity at the Eurozone level and, as a consequence, of automatic fiscal stabilisers able to cope with cyclical fluctuations;
• the limited scope for market mechanisms to effect economic adjustment because of various structural rigidities, including sticky wages, a low propensity to migrate and a variety of institutional barriers to cross-border flows of labour and capital.

---

[1] Martin Feldstein, 'EMU and international conflict', *Foreign Affairs* (November/December 1997), www.foreignaffairs.com/articles/europe/1997-11-01/emu-and-international-conflict.

In concluding, Tobin writes: 'it may be that the challenge of adapting to an irreversible currency union will bring the farsighted building of institutions needed to make the experiment successful. For Europeans' sake, let's hope so' (Tobin, 2001, p. 33). His words suggest the key questions that this Element tries to answer. How and why does the euro fall short of being a 'genuine' currency or 'complete' form of EMU? What needs to be done to make EMU substantially more complete and why is there entrenched resistance to what might seem to be the obvious and necessary steps towards it?

Kenen (1992) offers an excellent overview of both what was agreed at Maastricht and the potential risks. Presciently, he noted two likely concerns around fiscal policy: the policy mix problem arising from national autonomy in setting the fiscal stance; and the solvency problems if one member's profligacy has effects on others. Kenen (1992, p. 107) concludes his analysis by observing that although he approved of the idea and the blueprint for the euro, 'the blueprint is imperfect and incomplete'. He further notes the many difficulties 'answered sensibly, though compromise sometimes triumphed over clarity'.

Kenen (1992, p. 107) also draws analogies with the United States, reminding readers that 'the Federal Reserve System was likewise a compromise, balancing the needs of an emerging continental economy with regional interests and concerns, and it took many years for the new institutions to solve the problems generated by the need for compromise'. He ends optimistically, again alluding to US experience, but with this warning: 'the speed of adaptation in Europe will depend critically on the further development of the Community as a political entity'. As Barry Eichengreen and Charles Wyplosz observe in an obituary for Kenen, who died in 2012 at a time when the problems of the euro were at their worst, 'more than any other economist, Peter understood that monetary union was a legal as well as an economic construct'.[2] In addition, he drew attention to its political nature and the still unresolved matter of how to complete it politically.

As noted, monetary integration draws on the notion of the OCA, an approach that, as its name implies, attempts to establish when it makes sense to form a currency union as opposed to sticking with separate currencies. Various criteria have been put forward to ascertain optimality in an extensive literature since Mundell (1961) introduced the concept. In practice, three questions arise: given the many criteria, does the balance of benefits and costs justify joining the currency union; are its design or institutions suited, or capable of being amended, to achieve something closer to optimality; and can the structures and political economy of the participating countries adapt to be a better fit with the partners in the union?

---

[2] Barry Eichengreen and Charles Wyplosz, 'Kenen on the euro', *Voxeu Column* (21 December 2012), https://voxeu.org/article/kenen-euro.

Many economists, especially in the United States, stressed that the basic tenets of OCA theory had been neglected in the way the euro was introduced (Krugman, 2012; Jonung and Drea, 2010; see also Papaconstantinou, 2019), while the interplay between politics and economics in launching the euro, too, is part of the story (Snaith, 2014). However, a counter-argument, well articulated by Barry Eichengreen (2014), is that OCA theory itself – much of which was set out in the 1960s – is now very dated and has not kept pace with the evolution of international finance. Others have also queried whether the conventional OCA framework is helpful for understanding the euro crisis or how best to deal with it. Certainly, the euro cannot just be seen as a currency switch because it entails so many other adjustments to economic policymaking.

Despite the many doomsayers and sceptics, the euro, somehow, came into being. To the surprise of no one who has followed European matters, it was a compromise (Pisani-Ferry, 2014), not least in lacking features normally associated with a currency area. Many mainstream economists remained sceptical about its prospects and critical of its design, and when problems arose, some were quick to predict its demise (Stiglitz, 2016). But it has, so far, weathered the worst of the storms to hit it.

3 Defining a Complete and Genuine Economic and Monetary Union

Against this backdrop of an EMU widely adjudged to be suboptimal, it ought to be straightforward to define a viable EMU and to give substance to the terms 'genuine' or 'complete' in relation to EMU. There are several distinct, though connected, ways in which the completeness of EMU can be assessed. A document commonly known as the *Four Presidents' Report* (European Council, 2012a) set out 'a vision for the future of the Economic and Monetary Union', proposing four building blocks for a more robust framework for the governance of EMU in the pursuit of a 'genuine' EMU:

- an integrated financial framework to ensure a financially stable system;
- an integrated budgetary framework with the dual aim of assuring fiscal discipline and developing new common fiscal policy instruments;
- an integrated economic policy framework able to promote growth, employment and competitiveness in a manner consistent with the smooth functioning of EMU;
- enhancement of democratic legitimation and channels of accountability, justified particularly by the loss of national autonomy in budgetary and other economic matters as a direct consequence of greater top-down constraints on economic decision-making.

The first building block can be interpreted as *banking union*, the second as *fiscal union* and the last as at least a form of *political union*, while the third building block can be viewed as an elaboration of mechanisms to coordinate national economies more effectively and more comprehensively. Proposals for developing each of these building blocks were subsequently presented in a 'blueprint' by the European Commission (2012) and taken further at the end of 2012 by the European Council (2012b). Both of these documents included proposals on sequencing the introduction of the new measures, although it is noteworthy that they are by no means identical in what they propose.

Jerry Cohen (1994) suggests a basis for a definition in more political terms: there needs to be a sufficiently powerful state that is 'willing and able to use its influence to keep a currency union functioning effectively' and 'a broader constellation of related ties and commitments sufficient to make the loss of monetary autonomy, whatever the magnitude of prospective adjustment costs, seem basically acceptable to each partner'. Suggestions for how to construct an EMU reflecting Cohen's principles are put forward in the Commission blueprint (European Commission, 2012, p. 11):

- 'all major economic and fiscal policy choices of its Member States should be subject to deeper coordination, endorsement and surveillance at the European level';
- 'an autonomous and sufficient fiscal capacity that allows the policy choices resulting from the coordination process [should] be effectively supported'; while
- a 'commensurate share of decisions with regard to revenue, expenditure and debt issuance should be subject to joint decision-making and implementation at the level of EMU'.

These are ambitious requirements, given the reluctance of Member States to cede key economic powers to the supranational level. An underlying difficulty is the perceived democratic deficit of the EU institutions and the lack of consensus on how to redress it (Schmidt, 2020). No economic policy is devoid of distributive effects, though some are generally accepted to be more susceptible to them than others. Competition policy, for which the EU level has a prominent role, tends to be regarded as less politically sensitive, while monetary policy is in the middle of the spectrum. However, fiscal policy is often considered to be at the heart of the 'contract' between citizens and the state, and to need more visible democratic legitimation.

3.1 Membership

A very obvious sense in which EMU is incomplete is in having only nineteen members out of the twenty-seven in the EU. There is little need to dwell on why this has arisen. On the one hand, would-be members had to pass qualifying tests – the well-known convergence criteria – which, although interpreted rather flexibly, have slowed accession in some cases. On the other hand, the Maastricht Treaty provisions for an opt-out allowed the UK and Denmark to remain outside, while the other non-participating countries are formally in derogation of their obligation to become members. Sweden, following rejection of monetary union in its (non-binding) 2003 referendum established a de facto political veto, despite not having an opt-out.

Shortly after acceding to the EU in 2004, several of the then new members, such as Poland, seemed to be keen, and on track, to join the euro, but chose not to rush until the real economy shock of membership had been accommodated. Yet their enthusiasm faded as they realised the ramifications of the financial and sovereign debt crises. Even so, both Slovenia (2007) and Slovakia (2009) successfully acceded to the euro before the sovereign debt crisis struck, although for the latter the obligation to contribute to the Greek bailout caused political turmoil.

In contrast to the currency boards operated by the three Baltic Member States, Poland, the Czech Republic and Hungary had adopted inflation-targeting monetary regimes. Like Sweden, this meant that they could not enter the exchange rate mechanism (ERM II) – set up as a form of 'waiting-room' for euro adoption – because this would have entailed switching from inflation targeting to exchange rate targeting. For the Baltic states, having sustained a fixed exchange rate since 1992 – initially vis-à-vis the German mark and subsequently against the euro – the transition was more straightforward. Successively, Estonia (2011), Latvia (2014) and Lithuania (2015) joined.

Since then, euro area enlargement has stalled. However, the dynamics could change sooner rather than later. In July 2020, Bulgaria and Croatia joined Denmark as members of ERM II, and Croatia is now on track to join in 2023. Bulgaria wants to follow, keen to escape what some have called the 'purgatory' of being in a fixed exchange rate system with few of the benefits of full membership. Romania may be next in line. Marek Belka, formerly President of the National Bank of Poland, suggested in 2020, in his response to the survey, that Bulgaria and Croatia 'are no longer a matter of speculation', a proposition echoed by many other respondents. Belka also says that 'if inflation spikes in Poland, it may reconsider its position' and believes that the Czech Republic 'will follow suit'.

3.2 Common Policies

Being complete requires a policy framework that is able to act in the collective interest and, where necessary, to reconcile competing national interests, demands or preferences. In EMU, this has proved easier in some respects than others. Monetary policy had clear collective objectives and an explicit mandate, whereas fiscal policy and wider economic coordination were more diffuse.

The fundamental challenge facing EMU has been neatly explained by three senior European Commission Directorate-General for Economic and Financial Affairs (DG Ecfin) officials as an 'unsustainable equilibrium' made up of incomplete financial union, inadequate adjustment mechanisms and the lack of a central fiscal stabilisation function (Buti et al., 2018). Prior to the pandemic, it was an equilibrium in the sense that the existential threats to the euro had abated and there have been improvements in most of the relevant macroeconomic indicators. However, there is little doubt that the fiscal framework remains unsatisfactory and could face renewed turbulence in the aftermath of the pandemic and in light of events in Ukraine, in spite of the extensive reforms already enacted.

3.2.1 Monetary Policy

The aims of monetary policy are set out in the Treaty, emphasising a primary goal of assuring price stability. The institutional structure was also clearly specified, with the ECB at the apex of the European System of Central Banks (ESCB), in which the national central banks retain various responsibilities. However, monetary policy is unambiguously delegated to the ECB, with decisions taken by its Governing Council.

The ECB's 'two-pillar' approach to monetary policy was strongly influenced by Otmar Issing, the German member of its Executive Board. The first pillar was to monitor the growth of the money supply – a long-standing element of German monetary policy. The second pillar is more relevant to the short term and consists of leading indicators and measures of inflation expectations. In the words of Issing et al. (2001, p. 90), 'the range of relevant indicators, and their relative importance, change over time. Consequently, there is no permanently valid way to organise the assessment in a logically consistent manner.' In 2003, the first and second pillars were reversed, suggesting that the monetary pillar was being downgraded in importance, although Issing et al. (2001, p. 107) had explained that the separation between first and second pillar should be seen mainly as an 'organisational framework to structure the available information, both internally and for the benefit of the public'.

Price stability was not initially defined, but a subsequent clarification was that it was to mean close to, but below, 2 per cent inflation, as measured by the harmonised consumer price index. In contrast to the Bank of England, given a target of 2 per cent inflation but with a range of plus or minus one percentage point, the ECB could not be considered strictly to be engaged in inflation targeting. On the whole, ECB monetary policy has functioned effectively, although in the decade after the financial crisis, annual inflation averaged just 1.2 per cent, well below target. From the outset, the monetary policy of the ECB faced some criticism because it takes too little account of national circumstances, even though, as the single central bank, it can prescribe only one monetary policy for the entire euro area.

In line with its treaty mandate, ECB policy ostensibly prioritised price stability, although some academic analyses (see Gorter et al., 2008; Belke and Klose, 2013) suggested that the actual policy decisions were not that different from what would have happened had the ECB been required, as was the Federal Reserve, to take account of the unemployment rate. Nevertheless, as representatives of the Fed observe (see, for example, Bernanke, 2015), a legal obligation to fulfil a dual mandate of stabilising both prices and the real economy does affect the reasoning and hence the actions of decision-makers.

However, it is in its reluctance to embrace the wider economic governance role of other central banks that the ECB was subject to most criticism, a good example being lending in the last resort. Central banks have long been somewhat coy about whether it is something they formally do, but the ECB is more constrained than most because of the restrictions written into the Treaty. It has certainly been willing to inject substantial amounts of liquidity, particularly after the middle of 2007, to support the financial system, but has been inhibited from lending directly in the last resort to sovereigns. For De Grauwe (2013), this does not make sense because banks and sovereigns face similar risks of illiquidity that should be countered by lending in the last resort to both, not just to the banks.

With a Governing Council made up of the President and five other Executive Board members, plus the Governors of the central banks of all the countries participating in the euro, the core decision-making body of the ECB is unwieldy compared with the monetary policy committees of the other major currencies. This became recognised as an impending complication as more members acceded to euro membership. The accession of Lithuania, the nineteenth member, to the euro area in 2015 triggered a change in the voting rights,[3] as envisaged by

---

[3] ECB, 'How voting rights rotate on the ECB Governing Council', *Deutsche Bundesbank* (19 September 2014), http://bit.ly/3io6kDl.

the Governing Council in a decision taken in December 2002, but this did not prevent the Governing Council from growing to twenty-one members.

3.2.2 Economic Policy and the Scope for Stabilisation

For economic policy – the 'E' in EMU – the institutional dimension is less well developed. The underlying principle was that fiscal policy and structural policies should remain the prerogative of national governments but that, according to article 121 of the Treaty on the Functioning of the European Union (TFEU), 'Member States shall regard their economic policies as a matter of common concern and shall coordinate them within the Council'. Abstracting from any debates about whether fiscal activism is desirable or not, two principal justifications for this policy assignment can be put forward.

The first concerns the nature of shocks to the economy: if a shock is asymmetric, affecting a single country, the policy response should be tailored to the country, whereas a symmetric shock should elicit a collective response. An asymmetric shock can be dealt with either by using fiscal policy to offset the shock or by vertical intergovernmental fiscal flows to or from a higher level of government. Symmetric shocks, by contrast, call either for action by the higher level or for effective coordination of responses by all participating countries.

The second reason for the policy assignment is more overtly political: the EU (and, in the current stage of development, even less so the Eurozone) is not a federal entity. The great bulk of taxation and public expenditure remains at the Member State level and the choices involved are at the core of political contestation. Moreover, there is no prospect for the foreseeable future of much change, in spite of regular demands for the EU to act.

Coordination of structural policies, especially those affecting labour markets and product markets, was also in place based on article 145 of the TFEU. Yet, as Hodson (2011) shows, the overall impact of all these provisions was a disappointment. Attempts were made during the 2000s to launch strategies aimed at boosting growth and employment, eventually being brought together with broad economic policy guidelines issued by the European Commission. In quick succession, the EU adopted the European Employment Strategy (1997), the Lisbon Strategy (2000) with its now infamous goal of making the EU the 'most competitive and dynamic knowledge-based economy in the world' by 2010 and a Sustainable Development Strategy (2001) bringing together economic, social and environmental goals.

Despite relaunches and reconfigurations of these strategies, culminating in their integration into the Europe 2020 strategy launched in 2010, with its *leitmotiv* of 'smart, sustainable and inclusive growth', even their staunch supporters would now concede that these various forms of policy coordination had disappointed. The 'Green Deal' at the heart of the von der Leyen Commission's objectives can be seen as the latest attempt to create a strategic economic approach.

3.3 The Fiscal Framework

Unsurprisingly, there are diverse views on the core objectives of an EU fiscal framework, and this lack of consensus also feeds into ambiguity about what fiscal union might mean. It is therefore worth considering a number of likely components. A first is policy coherence: aggregate fiscal policy at the EU/Eurozone level has to act alongside monetary policy, while avoiding damaging spillover effects from policy conducted in one Member State to others. There are conflicting views and evidence on the magnitude and significance of such spillovers, but they are non-negligible. Fiscal policy interventions, as was so evident during the pandemic and previously during the sovereign debt crisis, are also needed to mitigate extreme events, such as the surge in inflation in 2022.

Second, a fiscal framework has to enable fiscal policy to contribute to the control, but also the sharing, of domestic risks. On the one hand, fiscal discipline is associated with the sustainability of public finances, including taking account of intergenerational fairness in the long term, as well as short-term stability. On the other hand, fiscal policy has a role in mitigating shocks to the economy as a whole or to parts of it that are subject to idiosyncratic shocks. The discipline motive calls for rules, whereas discretion may be needed for risk mitigation.

The EU's Stability and Growth Pact (SGP) – with its initially simple rules, even if widely misunderstood to mean keeping deficits to 3 per cent of gross domestic product (GDP), rather than 'close to balance or in surplus' – sought both to constrain the fiscal positions of EU Member States and to exert a degree of fiscal discipline. But the interplay between enforcement and compliance was neglected: as Papaconstantinou (2019, p. 20) notes, rules 'are there until events dictate that they have to be broken or, at the very least, circumvented'. The SGP was, and remains, at the heart of the rules-based approach adopted for EMU, and has been complemented by other rules at both national and EU levels, resulting in an increasingly complex, but also opaque system.

There is now a broad consensus on the need for these rules to be simplified and better tailored to a world of low interest rates and slower growth. A complex handbook – known as the *Vade Mecum* and running to some 220 pages in the 2018 edition, although a year later, perhaps in response to intensifying criticism, down to a mere 208 pages (European Commission, 2018b, 2019) – explains how EU fiscal rules are to be interpreted and applied. The Commission has also issued guidance notes (European Commission, 2015a), including on circumstances in which rules can be overridden. They include a downturn in the economy (either common or confined to one or a few members), allowance for certain forms of investment and 'major' structural reforms. In 2020, once the magnitude of the pandemic-related economic downturn became clear, the general escape clause was triggered, with restoration of these rules now expected only in 2023.

An altogether different function of fiscal policy is, as noted, enacting voters' preferences on the mix of spending commitments and taxes. Where rules constrain governments – even if for sound economic reasons – and external agencies limit government autonomy, democratic legitimation suffers, especially if the costs of adjustment are perceived as falling unfairly. This distributive issue is especially pronounced for fiscal policy because the state uses force to take from some and give to others. After the euro crisis, scrutiny clearly became more intense, both domestically (with the advent of fiscal councils required under the EU Fiscal Compact) and from the supranational level, notably through the EU's semester process. Yet little has been done to enhance legitimation.

While, in some cases, these scrutiny processes force governments to confront the hard choices they are prone to avoid, they also give rise to two sorts of political backlash. One is how the national authorities react, often portraying the external body (be it the European Commission or a fiscal watchdog) as the scapegoat for unpopular policies. Where this leads to better policy choices, it can be helpful, but a parallel phenomenon is governments seeking to gain popular credit by defiance, potentially leading to an erosion of commitment. The other is that public opinion becomes distanced from, and disenchanted with, EU norms and mechanisms, fuelling populism.

3.4 Governance Mechanisms, Ideas and Ideologies

'You cannot run a single currency on the basis of rules and statistics alone. It needs constant political assessment, as the basis of new economic, fiscal and social policy choices.'

– Jean-Claude Juncker[4]

From the outset, the euro was bedevilled by differences about what its conceptual and, indeed, ideological basis was or should be. These differences arose from distinct approaches to economic management, rooted in decades of post-war experience, not least, as Pisani-Ferry (2014) explains, the incompatible views of France and Germany. Two rather oddly named camps had formed in the debates around the Maastricht Treaty: the 'economists' and the 'monetarists'.

---

[4] European Commission, 'State of the Union 2018', https://ec.europa.eu/info/strategy/strategic-planning/state-union-addresses/state-union-speeches/state-union-2018_en.

They had divergent views on how to engineer the transition to the single currency, with the former arguing for a gradualist approach while the latter wanted a form of 'big bang'. In the end it was something of a compromise between the two.

What is meant by the term 'governance', particularly in the EU or Eurozone context, has never been precise or unambiguous, and it is telling that in some languages, such as German or Finnish, there is not an exact translation. As Tsoukalis (2016, pp. 193–4) rather pointedly puts it: governance, more so when qualified by the adjective 'European', is a 'term ambiguous enough to allow room for different interpretations (hence, perhaps its growing popularity)'. It is, in part, about how 'rules, process and behavior affect how powers are exercised at European level, particularly as regards openness, participation, accountability, effectiveness and coherence', a definition that hints at some of the democratic dilemmas now exercising Europe's elites.[5]

It is also about the incentives for policy choices that strike an appropriate balance between the interests of each Member State and the collective interest. Clearly, too, it is about how to go about correcting the flaws in the architecture of EMU. There are presumed disjunctions between the interests of core and periphery, or of large and small members. Brunnermeier et al. (2016, p. 4) portray the clash concisely: 'the basic elements of the contrasting philosophies can be delineated quite simply. The northern vision is about rules, rigor, and consistency, while the southern emphasis is on the need for flexibility, adaptability, and innovation. It is Kant versus Machiavelli.' However, core–periphery, North–South, Club Med and similar labels can often be not just misleading but also analytically dubious in implying that geography, per se, is a relevant, enduring and central influence.

Other debates have concerned the need for a centralised fiscal stabilisation capacity (included in the Werner, 1970, blueprint for EMU, but discarded by the late 1980s – Delors, 1989), the case for more explicit coordination mechanisms or the necessity of an economic counterpart to the powerful, centralised monetary authority. For some, the notion of the ECB on a pedestal at the heart of the governance system is seen as regrettable.

A mistake too often made by commentators from other parts of the world is to misunderstand the political economy constraints inherent in a union that falls well short of federal. Assertions along the lines of 'Europe should . . .' or 'the solution is . . .' followed by a proposal for a centralisation of governance mechanism or (in the case of Greece) for an exit from the euro neglect awkward political realities. These realities include the limited appetite for cross-border

---

[5] European Commission, European Governance, A White Paper, COM (2001) 428 final, Brussels, 25.07.2001.

solidarity, not least in a country such as Germany where the heavy cost of transforming the former Deutsche Demokratische Republik (DDR) is still fresh in the collective memory. Similarly, few Greeks think a return to the drachma would be an advance and would, instead, be likely to inhibit the reforms the country needs. Abstract economic analyses and propositions will only become viable once these political impasses are resolved, and the disagreements about the best solutions are only partly about clashes between competing schools of economic thought, be they 'German', 'Keynesian', 'Anglo-Saxon' or 'ordo-liberal'.

Implementation and compliance have been the enduring bugbears of EMU governance, not least because they are vulnerable to changing political winds and shifts in the balance of power, especially between larger Member States and the EU institutions. Heipertz and Verdun (2010, p. 204), writing before the euro crisis erupted, concluded that, 'on its own, the Commission cannot defend the SGP against the national interests of Germany and France' and went on to assert that German priorities, in particular, will be crucial in determining the approach to compliance.

Examination of the summer 2016 episode concerning Portugal and Spain suggests that they were prescient. In the Kafkaesque world of EMU, there will have been little surprise at the headline of a Council of Ministers press release on 8 August 2016, stating that the 'Council agrees to zero fines and new deadlines for Portugal and Spain'. Both countries were also spared a suspension of all or part of their entitlements to receipts from the EU's Structural and Investment Funds. Leaving aside the semantic matter of whether a fine of zero is a fine at all, the way the decision was justified is revealing. Spain and Portugal were found in mid-July to have done too little to rein in their excessive deficits and should, consequently, have been fined under the revised rules of the SGP, especially as a key element of the revision was to make the sanctions more credible.

Portugal, as the Council decision recalled,[6] had been in the excessive deficit procedure since 2009 and was initially obliged to correct its deficit by 2013. However, after it was accorded a bailout in 2011, subsequent Council decisions gave it more time to do so. For Spain, the Council noted the recovery of growth in the economy since 2013 and concluded that 'exceptional economic circumstances that would warrant a reduction of the amount of the fine do not exist'. Yet, in paragraphs 10–16 of the decision, the Council asserted that the efforts being made to transform the economy were enough to warrant cancellation of the fine.

---

[6] https://data.consilium.europa.eu/doc/document/ST-11553-2016-INIT/en/pdf.

Moreover, if reports in the German press are to be believed, the normally hard-line German Finance Ministry lobbied for the clemency shown to the two Iberian countries. Indeed, criticism of the decision in Germany focussed on the role behind the scenes of Wolfgang Schäuble, usually thought of as a fiscal hawk and a stickler for rules, in opposing fines. It is easy to dismiss this incident either as trivial or as an outbreak of common sense in which ill-conceived rules, sensibly, were overridden: in short, pragmatism. But an underlying question of the credibility of governance has to be confronted: if rules are in place but ignored when they become inconvenient, do they retain any value? It is already a piece of conventional wisdom that letting off Germany and France in 2003 paved the way for others to flout the SGP.

3.5 Internationalisation

A further dimension of being the complete currency of an advanced economy would be its extensive use internationally, but the euro plainly lacks the clout of the dollar. In charting the internationalisation of the euro, Cohen (2015, pp. 117–21) argues that it peaked very quickly, in 2003/4. Noting the euro being used mainly in neighbouring or associated countries and in relatively few segments of finance, he offers a number of explanations, but his core message is that the euro is 'a currency, in effect without a country'. Without attributes characterising a state, he claims, the euro will inevitably struggle to gain ascendancy in international finance because outsiders consider the currency 'only as good as the political agreement underlying it'. In this regard, disputes among Member States, and they are legion, are a significant barrier to internationalisation, even if the economic obstacles are tackled.

More recently, Cohen (2018, p. 1) was, if anything, even more dismissive, saying 'today, the world's major example of monetary rivalry is the emerging competition between the US dollar, long the dominant currency in the global economy, and the Chinese yuan'. Yet the evidence suggests otherwise, as the euro is comfortably the second most used currency for international reserves, while the renminbi is hampered not only by constraints on its convertibility and market concerns about financial stability but also by increased anti-China sentiment.

The EU's appetite for enhanced internationalisation of the euro has been a tricky matter over the years. The ECB has been reluctant to push it, whereas the Commission – especially recently, see European Commission (2018a) – has come to see it as a priority. Could an upsurge in disenchantment with the policies and dependability of the United States open a door for the euro? For this to happen, a number of conditions (Buti, 2020) would need to be met, a critical one among which is resolving the shortcomings in governance.

3.6 Legitimacy

In addition to contested ideas about the economics of EMU, the legitimacy of policy actions undertaken in the governance of the euro has elicited diverse concerns from political scientists. The increasingly complex rules and the difficulty in changing them when they manifestly become ill-suited to a new economic context pose a particular challenge. The problem is aggravated when one-size-fits-all rules make little sense if some of the key economic parameters – growth rates, scale and maturity of the debt burden – are so different among Eurozone members.

The result is a combination of mistrust and dissatisfaction inimical to a shared sense of legitimacy. On the one hand, bending rules to achieve necessary flexibility to cope with unforeseen circumstances was anathema to one group of countries. On the other, the mechanisms for change were too limited to react either adequately or quickly, leading to a loss of trust in policymakers, and often implemented by 'stealth' rather than transparent and accountable means (Schmidt, 2020; Papaconstantinou, 2019). Then, EU actors risk alienating all sides: as Schmidt (2020, p. 9) puts it, 'Southern Europeans continue to feel oppressed even when accommodated, while Northern Europeans feel deceived regardless.' These sentiments resurfaced in the debates around how Europe should respond to the pandemic and were again visible in the reacting to the Russian invasion of Ukraine.

The mistrust goes both ways: according to Sinn (2014, p. 17), the 'animosity Germany faces in western Europe is stronger than anything the country has experienced since World War II'. Yet, Schimmelfennig (2015, p. 192) refers to the difficult interstate bargaining as a 'chicken game' in which saving the euro is crucial, but so too is avoiding paying the price of adjustment – Eurozone changes in response to the sovereign debt crisis 'largely follow the preferences of Germany, the country with superior bargaining power'.

A successful euro is, however, also at the heart of the European integration 'project', and assessments of it as a political project for many participants go well beyond an economic cost–benefit analysis. Ironically, the two countries undertaking the most comprehensive assessments of the *economic* case for joining, Sweden and the UK, then used these studies to stay out. The political imperative is captured in a speech by Angela Merkel to the Bundestag on 19 May 2010 (defending the first Greek bailout): '[I]f the euro fails, Europe fails. This must not happen'; it is a sentiment she has expressed repeatedly. In an echo she might not wholly welcome, Yannis Varoufakis, Greek Finance Minister in the early days of the Syriza government, said on BBC *This Week* on 1 June 2018: 'The Eurozone is the core of the European Union and the euro is a currency designed to fail, not intentionally, unintentionally perhaps. And if the euro fails, the European Union is gone.'

4 The Euro in Its Third Decade: From Crisis to Serenity . . . and Back?

The euro has, in Jean Pisani-Ferry's words, been through '10 quiet years followed by 10 tumultuous ones' (Pisani-Ferry, 2018, p. 1). Early in the tumultuous decade, its very existence was called into question. Having attained the age of twenty-one, the euro should now be mature. Yet it continues to be bedevilled by doubts about its durability, resilience and ability to cope with the constraints of operating without a true state behind it.

The economic performance of members of the Eurozone pre-pandemic, simply measured by total GDP growth between 2000 and 2019, provides one measure of the impact of EMU. The Eurozone as a whole grew in this period by just over a quarter, slightly less than for the EU28. However, the aggregate disguises very diverse trends. At one extreme, Ireland (a member from the outset), the three Baltic countries (acceding only in the 2010s), Malta (2008) and Slovakia (2009) have seen their economies double in size over the twenty years (Figure 1). At the other, Greece (from 2001) and Italy (a founder member) have seen almost no growth, Portugal achieved just 14.2 per cent, and the countries many would regard as the core founder members (Belgium, Germany, France, Austria and the Netherlands) ranged from 27 per cent (Germany) to 34.6 per cent (Belgium). Only Luxembourg of the traditional core – an economy with a very large financial sector – stands out with growth of 68.8 per cent.

The two decades, manifestly, cover a plethora of ups and downs. Greece ostensibly fared well prior to 2009, although with hindsight it was macroeconomically

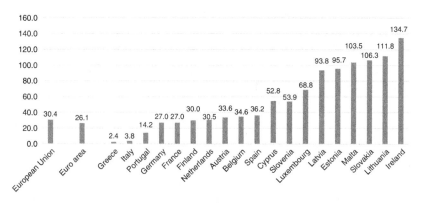

Figure 1 GDP growth of Eurozone members, 2000–19 (percentage)
Source: Own elaboration from Ameco database.

unsustainable growth and the years of decline during the 2010s were brutal, whereas Italy has stagnated throughout, exceeding 2 per cent annual growth just once (in 2002, when growth attained 3.8 per cent). Germany in the early years of the euro was seen as a laggard country, even being labelled by the *Economist* magazine in July 1999 the 'sick man of the euro' before this dubious title was switched in May 2005 to Italy, 'the real sick man of Europe'. It is also disingenuous to infer, as too many commentators are prone to do, causality: yes Italy's economy has stagnated during its membership of the Eurozone, but there are many other reasons for it which successive governments have been unable to counter.

4.1 The Rollercoaster of Crises

The extent of the problems encountered after 2007 exposed major governance failings. These have been analysed exhaustively and have led to a series of reforms, across the spectrum of governance. They have encountered resistance and, in many (if not most) instances, what emerged falls short of the ambitions at the outset. There are two principal explanations for the euro crisis: for some commentators it was the result of policy failures; for others, flaws in the design of the euro meant that problems were inevitably going to arise.

Those that question the design cast doubt on many different characteristics, including the manner in which responsibility for different areas of policy is divided and the unresolved issue of how much political union is feasible. Today, the flaws in the design and governance of the euro are reasonably well understood, despite continuing disputes about how best to correct them. They include institutional weaknesses, a lack of crucial policy instruments and a failure by most governments to understand that being part of an EMU is not compatible with a 'business-as-usual' approach to economic policymaking. Because the instruments for the coordination of national economic policies are mainly 'soft', there is, too, an 'unresolved contradiction between a full integration of monetary policy and a weak integration of other economic policies' (Jabko, 2015, p. 71).

When the newly elected PASOK government in Greece announced in October 2009 that its budget deficit was going to be far higher than previously signalled, there was no inkling that it would turn into an existential crisis for the euro. Although the global financial crisis wreaked havoc in the financial sector, with especially severe consequences for Ireland, and saw a sharp contraction in GDP in a number of countries, there were signs of recovery as early as the summer of 2009. Some EU Member States, such as Spain and France, were seduced into thinking that their tighter prudential controls on banks had spared them from the financial crisis afflicting the 'Anglo-Saxon' world. Germany returned to growth in the third quarter of 2009, pulling the Eurozone with it.

4.2 Causes of Crisis

The subsequent euro crisis arose, according to Rehn (2020), who was in the hot seat at the time as European Commissioner for Economic and Financial Affairs, for several reasons:

- the severity and diversity of macroeconomic imbalances
- the doom-loop linking banks and sovereigns
- neglect of financial stability
- the absence of firefighting tools in the Maastricht framework.

To the last of these could be added the misplaced belief that such tools were not needed, so long as policy actors did 'the right thing'. Few today would subscribe to that view. Certainly, market pressures played a pivotal role in triggering the euro crisis, but it is far from obvious that governments are left at the mercy of markets. On the contrary, in his lively account of the crisis, Paul Wallace (2016, p. 243) argues that the 'capacity of bond markets to shake governments had defined the acute phase of the euro crisis. Led above all by the Fed, however, central banks had humbled the bond vigilantes by making massive interventions across the yield curve. In this new era, it was investors who now quailed at the power of central banks.'

However, there is a rather more conventional explanation for the euro crisis: a failure to control debt, especially financed from abroad (Baldwin and Giavazzi, 2015, p. 19). In several Eurozone countries, either private or public debt – and, in some cases, both – grew to unsustainable levels. The direct result was a widening of macroeconomic imbalances, especially visible in the current account of the balance of payments, but also in property markets. In Ireland and Cyprus, both hit by banking crises requiring bailouts, the ratio of banking assets to GDP had spiralled to multiples of GDP.

As Rehn explains it, the euro endured a crisis in three stages: the prologue was the fallout from the sub-prime crisis in the United States; there was then an intense sovereign debt crisis from late 2009 to 2011, but one broadly confined to smaller members and thus manageable; and it became a true systemic crisis as Italy and Spain were nearly engulfed and even France came under strain. The response became a balancing-act between extinguishing bush-fires threatening to escalate out of control and, at the same time, reforming the EMU architecture. The tension between the two and the entrenched differences among the leading actors on how to proceed accentuated the challenges of arriving at a genuine EMU. In particular, incompatibilities between the German government, the International Monetary Fund (IMF) and the ECB – the three sources of funds to mitigate the crisis – led to a narrow range of areas on which they could agree to act: 'an impossible triangle', according to Rehn (2020, p. 12). The consequence was the politically feasible routinely dominating the economically optimal.

Baldwin and Giavazzi (2015) point to a number of what they call 'amplifiers' of the initial problems. The treaty prohibition on the ECB acting as a lender of last resort meant, first, that governments had nowhere to turn when faced with a credit crunch, in contrast to the ability of other central banks, such as the Fed or the Bank of England, to 'print' money. Second, the predominance of bank financing and the relatively weak capital base of the banks in a number of countries left them vulnerable to an upsurge in non-performing loans. Also, as Aizenmann (2016, p. 11) explains, closer financial integration can be disruptive: 'unlike commercial trade, inter-temporal trade of financial assets may lead to growing exposure to abrupt reversal of flows over time, thus testing the viability of a shallow currency area'. He also argues that severe asymmetric shocks can detract from the benefits of currency union over time unless there is closer integration and pooling of insurance mechanisms – see also Schelkle (2018).

A third amplifier was, again, the 'doom-loop' between banks and sovereigns. In contrast to earlier centuries when banks feared sovereign default, the state has increasingly become the ultimate guarantor of banks. The 'too big to fail' phenomenon can, in turn, lead to risky behaviour and inadequate control (de Larosière et al., 2009) by senior management of poorly understood financial instruments. Fragmentation of financial services among Eurozone members exacerbated these risks and the case for EU-level prudential supervision was already being made before the sovereign debt crisis (Begg, 2009).

Interest spreads between sovereigns are shown in an updated version (highlighting the dramatic changes between the collapse of Lehman Brothers in September 2008 and the 'whatever it takes' speech by Mario Draghi in July 2012) of a chart that became iconic for explaining what went wrong (Figure 2). Spreads had declined virtually to nothing by the mid-2000s, but they then diverged sharply before decreasing again as the Greek crisis receded.

The European Commission (2012) argued that market discipline had been found wanting and its analysis pointed the finger at a range of other institutional shortcomings, as a paragraph from the analysis explains:

> By the time of the eruption of the financial crisis in 2008 some euro area Member States had accumulated large private and public debts, losses in competitiveness, and macroeconomic imbalances. This rendered them particularly vulnerable when the crisis struck, with considerable contagion effects across the euro area once it turned into a sovereign debt crisis. The build-up of these vulnerabilities was partly due to an insufficient observance of and respect for the agreed rules underpinning EMU as laid down in the

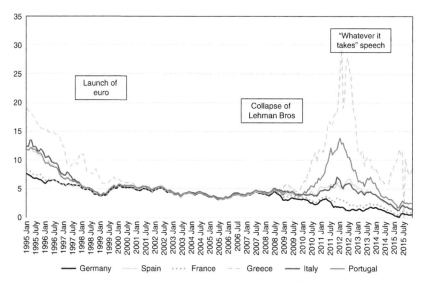

Figure 2 Interest spreads in the Eurozone
Source: Own elaboration, using data from the ECB.

> Stability and Growth Pact (SGP). In good part these vulnerabilities stemmed
> from features of the original institutional setup of EMU, in particular the lack
> of a tool to address systematically macroeconomic imbalances.
>
> (European Commission, 2012, p. 1)

Too little was done to counter widening gaps between countries in competitiveness, and too little account was taken of the potentially damaging effects of
spillover from one country to another. The extent and implications of financial
market integration for the sustainability of national public finances in vulnerable countries and the scope for contagion across borders were overlooked. The
Commission, correctly, noted the asymmetry between having regulation and
prudential supervision predominantly at the national level, and the markets and
associated risks increasingly at the supranational level. Mervyn King, former
Governor of the Bank of England, summed up the dilemma for the authorities:
'global banks are global in life, but national in death' (quoted by the BBC,
18 March 2009).[7]

4.3 Flexibility

The comparative rigidity of the supply side of the economy in many of the
countries worst affected by the crisis also played a role. Because devaluation is

---

[7] Steve Schifferes, 'Can banking regulation go global?' *BBC News* (18 March 2009), http://news
.bbc.co.uk/1/hi/business/7950758.stm.

no longer an option in a currency union, other policy instruments have to be used to adjust an economy hit by any kind of shock. Under EMU, fiscal policy is also constrained by the SGP and other commitments, so that more of the burden of adjustment necessarily falls on structural policies (Ardy et al., 2006). The expression 'internal devaluation' came to be used to describe this sort of policy response and has been associated above all with pressures to reduce wages, but the more fundamental question is whether the economy is sufficiently able to adjust. Product market regulation, the quality of public administration and a variety or other determinants often exert a stronger influence on flexibility.

Structural reforms can, over time, improve the resilience of economies to shocks and lead to enhanced flexibility. But they are often unpopular, result in losses for some favoured interests and take time to bear fruit. Hence, politicians will be loath to enact them for the simple political economy reason that they will be held responsible for the pain, while their successors enjoy the gains. It is little wonder that politicians find it easy to neglect reform in these circumstances, and sometimes even rewarding to shift blame for unpopular policies to 'Brussels' or 'Frankfurt'. In any case, as the contributions to Campos et al. (2018) show, the idea that such reforms offer a panacea is misplaced: much more subtlety is needed about what to do and how to sequence them.

The incentives to engage in structural reforms should be greater after joining a monetary union, according to the literature surveyed by Leiner-Killinger et al. (2007), but a short-term decline in interest rates on joining a currency union may deter such action. Sharply falling costs of public debt service mean that more heavily indebted states obtain a windfall gain equivalent to several percentage points of GDP. As Figure 3 shows, the gains for Italy and Greece in the period from 1995 to 2005 were of the order of six percentage points of GDP, while Belgium (also highly indebted) saw its debt service charge fall by more than four percentage points of GDP.

Yet one reading of what has happened in the Eurozone is that, with the windfall gains now fully used up, the original logic of the necessity of structural reforms now applies with even greater force for those countries that delayed them in the first place. The pressure exerted on the Greek, Italian and, later, French governments to bolster such reforms is arguably greater because of their previous reluctance to take the hard choices.

4.4 Imbalances

Imbalances can arise between countries bilaterally or multilaterally, in the structure of an economy, or between short- and long-term imperatives. There are often two sides to imbalances and one of the most enduring challenges in economic policy

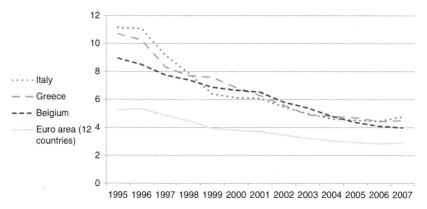

Figure 3 Windfall effect of joining the euro on debt service charges
(General government interest charges as a percentage of GDP, 1995–2007)
Source: Own elaboration from Ameco database.

coordination has been how to reduce existing asymmetries and introduce effective burden-sharing. It is also glaringly obvious that an external deficit will bite because the country will find it progressively harder to finance it, whereas a country in surplus can go on accumulating the resulting inflow of money with little direct pressure to correct the imbalance. If the result is too much demand being sucked out of the system into savings by the surplus countries, a reversion to past growth rates cannot be taken for granted. Yet, there are undeniable obstacles to more effective burden-sharing, aggravated by the fact that deficits are associated in public perceptions with recklessness and surpluses with virtue.

In a conventional monetary union, imbalances between regions are not generally regarded in the same way as the external imbalances of nations. Even if they could be accurately quantified, no one dwells on the trade deficits of Wallonia or Andalusia, or on whether Sicily, the Hauts de France region, California or Michigan has a balance of payments problem. This is not because such imbalances do not exist or have no consequences but because the means by which they are accommodated are different. A country with a persistent balance of payments deficit on current account has to finance it by attracting capital from abroad, so that if its capacity to borrow declines, it faces a crunch. Only the United States, benefiting from what Eichengreen (2011) – using Valéry Giscard d'Estaing's phrase – calls the 'exorbitant privilege' of issuing the globally accepted currency, is exempt. A region within a currency area adjusts through spending less, emigration of labour and some inflows of private capital (Goodhart, 1980).

The Eurozone as a whole has, until its recent shift into substantial surplus, had a current account position close to balance, unlike the United States (often with a sizeable deficit) or China with its substantial surpluses. To this extent, the

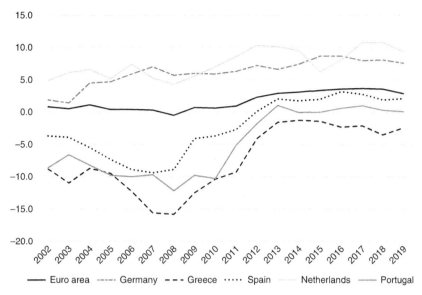

Figure 4 Current account of balance of payments, selected Eurozone countries
(percentage of GDP)
Source: Own elaboration from Ameco database.

Eurozone has not been a bad global citizen. However, the positions of individual
Member States became increasingly unbalanced during the first decade of the euro.
By 2008, the Spanish and Portuguese deficits had reached 10 per cent and more than
12 per cent, respectively, of GDP, and that of Greece 15 per cent – see Figure 4.
Much of the counterpart was in the rising German and Dutch surpluses.

A current account deficit is not intrinsically a problem, especially if it reflects
an inflow of capital being put to productive use, notably in growth-promoting
investment. However, deficits can be symptoms of a deeper pathology and
disparate national circumstances cannot be neglected. Thus, in Spain, a very
high investment rate in the mid-2000s (Ireland similarly) coincided with a huge
surge in investment in property. Figure 5 shows the share of gross fixed capital
formation (that is, investment) in the construction sectors of the Spanish and
Irish economies reaching a peak of more than 20 per cent of GDP in 2007,
before collapsing to below the euro area rate in the years of crisis.

4.5 Institutional Stresses and Shortcomings

There is a stark contrast between the very substantial powers delegated to the
ECB for the conduct of monetary policy and the much more limited capacity of
the EU or Eurozone institutions in relation to other economic policies.

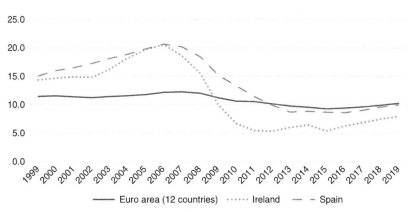

Figure 5 Gross fixed capital formation in construction (percentage of GDP)
Source: Own elaboration from Ameco database.

Moreover, the time taken to reach and implement decisions during the euro crisis tended to exacerbate the problems. Using a phrase borrowed from his former Bruegel colleague Nicolas Véron, Pisani-Ferry (2014) observed that the EU has an 'executive deficit' rooted in the shortcomings of these economic governance institutions, not least in lacking the means to manage crises. His analysis led to the conclusion that fair-weather mechanisms could not cope when the mercury dropped. But there was also uncertainty about where responsibilities lay for dealing with crises.

There are also tensions between the powers of Member States and those of the supranational level, with overlap in responsibilities prone to cause friction (Acocella, 2020). In the same vein, Hodson (2021, p. 272) argues that the sovereign debt crisis was deeper and lasted longer because of institutional politics, observing that a 'deficit of leadership in the early stages of the euro crisis deepened Greece's fiscal problems and caused the crisis to spread'. There is an elaborate process, now known as the 'semester', through which the supranational institutions seek to influence the conduct of national policies, but its effectiveness had been questioned prior to the pandemic (Darvas and Leandro, 2015; Efstathiou and Wolff, 2018). In particular, national policymakers have few incentives to take account of the cross-border consequences of decisions taken in response to domestic priorities.

Among many others, Pisani-Ferry (2014) is also robustly critical of the adequacy of annual monitoring, noting that Spain moved from an annual budget surplus in 2007 to a deficit in excess of ten percentage points of GDP just two years later. With hindsight, it is easy to see how reliance on the tax yield from overheating financial or construction sectors could lull finance ministries into complacency about public revenues, but the link between imbalances and fiscal sustainability was not convincingly made by those charged with macroeconomic surveillance. Nevertheless, signs of growing imbalances should have raised alarms.

In addition, as Pisani-Ferry recounts, the incomplete institutional structure had repercussions for international policy coordination:

> Tim Geithner, the U.S. Treasury Secretary in the first Obama administration, was very keen on keeping in touch with whoever matters in the economic and financial world. To this end, he frequently called and met foreign counterparts, officials of the International Monetary Fund, and major market participants, but when trying to get in touch with the euro area, he faced the famous (although wholly apocryphal) Henry Kissinger question: What is Europe's telephone number?
>
> Geithner's public record reveals the answer he found: from January 2010 to June 2012 he had 58 contacts with Jean-Claude Trichet and Mario Draghi, in their capacity of president of the European Central Bank, 36 with Wolfgang Schäuble, the German finance minister, 32 with successive French finance ministers, 11 with Olli Rehn, the European Commission's man for Economic and Monetary Affairs, a few others with the ministers of finance of the countries in crisis, and two only with his official counterpart Jean-Claude Juncker, then president of the Eurogroup.

He concludes that in 'the eyes of the U.S. government, the institutional body that matters in Europe is the ECB. Then come national governments, especially Germany and France. Then the Commission. And far behind, the man who supposedly embodies the role of euro-area finance minister.'

5 The Broadening EMU Governance Framework Assessed

'Standing still is the fastest way of moving backwards in a rapidly changing world.'
– Lauren Bacall

When the euro was launched, the institutions, rules and procedures behind its governance seemed relatively straightforward. The SGP was a simple rule, surveillance was light-touch, the ECB had a mandate to deliver price stability and did not aspire to take on other tasks, while regulation and supervision of financial intermediaries remained a national competence. Policy coordination, whether horizontally between fiscal and monetary policy or vertically between the national and supranational levels, was limited.

As the flaws in this framework became ever more apparent, a succession of reforms resulted in a much broader system of governance, with new institutions, more extensive rules and a recasting of responsibilities. Plans have abounded; some have been adopted, others discarded or left in the 'too difficult' box. Slowly and often painfully, however, the euro has become a more robust currency, remaining second only to the dollar in global importance. For an entire generation of citizens of the founding member countries, the lira, franc, peseta or schilling – though perhaps not quite yet the DM – are now historical curiosities found in grandparents' cupboards.

Yet differences of perspective – not least between France and Germany – already evident before the euro was launched go a long way to explain the subsequent inability to resolve the euro crisis in a timely manner. At the risk of oversimplification, these derive from incompatible views about whether there should be discretion in macroeconomic management – especially fiscal policy – or an insistence on adherence to rules. While France and Germany are manifestly pivotal actors, who leads the Eurozone is, as Puetter (2021) observes, still a question without a clear answer. Hodson (2011) believes that the Eurogroup has not evolved to become the leadership body some hoped.

Part of the problem was that it was not easy to understand why action to deal with the sovereign debt crisis took so long. One explanation, according to Jean Pisani-Ferry (2014, p. 53), was that

> Greece was the perfect culprit: after failing to join the euro during its launch in 1999 and having narrowly qualified in 2001, the country immediately began to exceed the budgetary deficit limits it had promised to stick to. It attempted to cover up the true state of its public finances, and was then forced to ask for help after being exposed.

He also poses the interesting question of what might have happened if Ireland had called for help sooner than Greece.

5.1 The Focus of Reforms

In response to the financial crisis, the initial focus of reforms was on improving the oversight of the financial sector. Subsequently, the most extensive efforts went on recasting fiscal governance alongside efforts to improve crisis management and resolution. Agreement of a *Fiscal Compact* and new provisions for advance scrutiny by the Commission of the annual budgets of Eurozone members (part of the 2013 'two-pack'), complementing a reformed SGP, were aimed at improving the sustainability of public finances. A new Macroeconomic Imbalances Procedure (MIP), modelled on the SGP in having preventive and corrective arms, sought to deter damaging imbalances other than in the public finances. The creation of the permanent European Stability Mechanism (ESM) in 2012 put in place a formal entity charged with assisting Eurozone members facing financing problems, albeit in an intergovernmental agreement among Eurozone members, not as an EU body.

Soon thereafter, establishing a banking union became the most pressing priority. In parallel, the ECB made a variety of changes to the way it contributes to economic governance, despite continuing to operate within an unchanged legal framework. Governance innovations included, notably, the advent of what is now known as the semester, the annual cycle of monitoring by and recommendations from the EU level for the conduct of national policies.

These changes were extensive, but are they enough? Some oft-discussed ideas showed little sign of progress. For example, as several of the contributors to Buti et al. (2020) discuss, neither a euro area Treasury nor a euro area finance minister seem likely soon. In the same volume (p. 7), Henrik Enderlein, noting the continuing vulnerabilities of the euro area, comes to a blunt conclusion about the many ambitions for enhancing the governance of EMU put forward in the plethora of reports and reviews of recent years:

> 'None of the big structural steps that were discussed since 2015 has been implemented. The euro area crisis is over. The quick-fix institutional framework that was built during the crisis is still in place and makes the euro area more stable. But we are far away from a more structurally sound EMU, encompassing fiscal union, banking union, and political union alongside monetary union.

If Enderlein is correct that the appetite for significant reforms is lacking outside periods of crisis, institutional and other gaps in the governance framework will persist. Care is also needed to prevent institutional hurdles from rendering what might be a good idea in theory incapable of being implemented in practice, or susceptible to being introduced only in a lowest common denominator form that undermines the very purpose of the change.

The handling of macroeconomic imbalances is a case in point. The MIP – at best – functions only indirectly and has manifestly failed to rein in the large current account surpluses of several northern Member States, most obviously Germany. Yet the easy retort from successive German finance ministers is hard to discredit: adjustment 'cannot take the form of successful countries voluntarily limiting their competitiveness' – Wolfgang Schäuble, speaking at the Brussels Economic Forum in 2011 (quoted in Rehn, 2020, p. 264). There may be ways to reduce the excessive savings of major surplus countries, but they are not easily codified in rules.

In a genuine EMU, the remit of institutions and mechanisms created in response to the financial/sovereign debt crises of the late 2000s may be ill-suited to broader governance aims. For example, the ESM, with its mandate to provide liquidity support to single Member States losing access to financial markets (subject to strict conditionality), was canvassed as a means of dealing with the much broader challenge of supporting a collective recovery from the pandemic. Even where appropriate technical solutions have been identified, their political acceptability is often in doubt and the normative dimension to the policy model at the heart of EMU cannot be ignored. Moreover, unless the challenges of implementation and compliance that have bedevilled EMU previously are overcome, even clever new mechanisms risk foundering.

5.2 An Evolving and Maturing Central Bank

There were credible explanations for the reluctance of the ECB to take on new governance roles. Writing in 2010, Hodson (2011, p. 135) noted that the ECB tended to regard measures to further European integration as 'subordinate to its preferences for price stability'. Given how the ECB has evolved over the years of crisis, his assertion would be much harder to defend today. The ECB has expanded its role in economic governance, not just in the immediate sense of additional responsibilities associated with prudential supervision at both the macro and the micro levels (which could be interpreted as a *functional broadening*) but also in the sense of a *deepening* in terms of having a generally more central and profound role in the overall conduct of economic policy.

From 2007 onwards, the ECB was often the only policy actor able to react quickly enough to prevent serious economic damage. This 'actor of first resort' role is one the ECB appeared uncomfortable with, prompting frequent calls for governments to take more responsibility. Nevertheless, the ECB has been forced to exercise a form of political leadership, a function tacitly accepted – indeed, welcomed – by other actors (Verdun, 2019), as well as becoming embroiled more heavily in governance, including as part of the 'troika' of institutions overseeing bailout programmes. As is now widely acknowledged, ECB President Mario Draghi's assertion that the ECB would 'do whatever it takes to preserve the euro' was a game changer; his follow-up sentence, 'And believe me, it will be enough', testified to a strong belief that the central bank had the power to do so.[8]

As contributors to the discussion in chapter 5 of Blinder et al. (2013) note, the development of the ECB has seen it become a more 'normal' central bank, closer to the pivotal governance roles of the Fed, the Bank of England or the Bank of Japan. In a felicitous phrase, Rehn (2020, p. 14) refers to the 'silent transformation of the ECB: from Buba to Fed'. Although its extended roles help to render EMU more 'genuine', they can also cause difficulties, not least for its independence, in the face of conflicting political demands from, and narratives within, member countries (Demetriades, 2020).

In January 2020, the ECB launched a review of its monetary policy strategy, the first since 2003, prompting a number of commentators to observe not only that it was overdue but that in future it should happen with greater frequency.

---

[8] Mario Draghi's 'Whatever it takes', YouTube, www.youtube.com/watch?v=tB2CM2ngpQg.

After wide-ranging consultations and debates, delayed by the pandemic, a revised strategy was agreed by the Governing Council on 8 July 2021,[9] in which the headline change was a shift to a 2 per cent symmetrical inflation target. This is similar to that of the Bank of England, but does not have the latter's ± one percentage point as a range; instead, the ECB will regard 'negative and positive deviations from this target as equally undesirable', but without a precise range. More account will be taken of housing costs, not included in the standard harmonised index of consumer prices.

While a two pillar approach is maintained, the monetary pillar has been broadened to become the 'monetary and financial analysis', reflecting a greater emphasis on financial stability. Noting that underlying changes in economies have reduced the scope for interest rates alone to enable the ECB to meet its objectives, the statement signals that other instruments will be needed: 'in particular forward guidance, asset purchases and longer-term refinancing operations, as appropriate'. The strategy will also involve paying some heed to how climate change affects economic activity, although, according to David Marsh and Danae Kyriakopoulou, 'the approach is focused on risk, with language about risks posed on finance by climate change, not the effect finance has on climate (the so-called double-materiality)'[10] and will disappoint climate activists.

Irrespective of its future monetary policy, the expansion of the ECB role makes it harder to argue that it should be seen as mainly a technocratic agency, to be judged on 'output legitimacy' terms because some of its expanded competence has distributive consequences (Chang, 2018). By implicitly acting as a lender of last resort, taking part in the troika and calling on governments to adopt discretionary fiscal policy, the ECB has become more political. According to Chang, there have also been several instances of the ECB writing to national governments to advocate policy changes. Yet its accountability arrangements and treaty base are little changed. The regular spats with assorted German interests and the ensuing cases submitted to the German Constitutional Court about the conduct of ECB policy testify to the tensions.

More recently, and especially after the May 2020 decision by the German Court on the legality of the Pandemic Emergency Purchase Programme (PEPP), the ECB has sought to engage with the Bundestag. Nevertheless, with the pandemic emergency seemingly abating, there have been further calls for the ECB to be restrained in revisiting its strategy. Thus, a group of German economists – none of whom would be regarded as outside the reasonable mainstream – published a policy note calling for fiscal dominance of monetary policy to be avoided and

---

[9] The ECB's monetary policy strategy statement, http://bit.ly/3H4eZFv.
[10] http://bit.ly/3ETXaGe.

for the hierarchy of objectives putting price stability first to be retained (Feld et al., 2021). They advocated keeping the inflation target at close to (but under) 2 per cent, but suggested looking at different measures of inflation and enhancing transparency. This, bluntly, is close to a demand to maintain the status quo ante prevailing prior to the pandemic.

As inflation surged in 2022, more so after the invasion of Ukraine, the ECB faced a quandary: vulnerabilities in highly indebted Eurozone countries militated against a rapid normalisation of monetary policy, yet there was a growing clamour in northern countries for action to curb rising prices. Other central banks were also caught out and it was only in the summer of 2022 that the ECB at last raised its benchmark rate – by 50 basis points to take it to just zero – several months after the Fed and the Bank of England. To allay the concerns of the South, a new transmission protection instrument was announced. Its purpose is stated on the ECB website as being to enable 'secondary market purchases of securities issued in jurisdictions experiencing a deterioration in financing conditions not warranted by country-specific fundamentals'.[11]

In practice, this means country-specific asset purchases, but, as David Marsh puts it, 'any limited scheme on bond purchases that would be acceptable to the Bundesbank and other more orthodox members of monetary union would run into strong opposition in Italy. And a framework that would meet the needs of Italy would fall foul of the Bundesbank.'[12] A polemical commentary by a group of prominent German economists, referring in its title to 'the ECB's toxic bond purchase[s]', quickly vindicated Marsh's conclusion.[13]

5.3 Banking Union

Of the areas highlighted in the *Four Presidents' Report* and the *Five Presidents' Report*, banking union has made the most progress. Major advances include the establishment of the ECB-led Single Supervisory Mechanism (SSM) and the Single Resolution Mechanism (SRM), and (at least prior to the pandemic) a significant cleaning-up of bank balance sheets. Yet, as Angeloni (2020) makes clear, a genuine banking union is far from being in place. Even in relation to supervision, he notes a number of shortcomings resulting from an absence of European law, obliging the ECB in its role as lead supervisor to rely on national laws. The latter can, and do, differ in ways that affect the exercise of supervisory and regulatory powers.

---

[11] The Transmission Protection Instrument, www.ecb.europa.eu/press/pr/date/2022/html/ecb .pr220721~973e6e7273.en.html.

[12] OMFIF, Eight thorny questions over ECB fragmentation, http://bit.ly/3gL24xs.

[13] Lars P. Feld, Clemens Fuest, Volker Wieland et al., The ECB's Toxic Bond-Purchase Program, Project Syndicate, http://bit.ly/3Uk1xQA.

A related legal complication is how the SSM and the SRM, as Eurozone entities, interact with other agencies bearing on banking union but affecting all Member States, such as the European Banking Authority or the European Systemic Risk Board (Ferran and Babis, 2015). There is, too, a question over voluntary participation in components of banking union by non-members of the Eurozone: Denmark and Sweden, for example, had shown some interest in joining, but have procrastinated. There is also ambiguity about the circumstances in which the public purse may be called upon in future to bail out systemically important banks. Prevention through more effective supervision is one answer, but some see the remedy in cutting banks down to size, such that they can fail without severe repercussions for the real economy, implying a challenge for competition policy as well as policy on financial stability. But the reality is that in most EU countries there are still banks big enough relative to the economy to be a threat, were they to collapse.

There is also a fuzzy boundary between significant banks (those capable of causing systemic problems and directly supervised by the ECB, under the SSM) and the rest of the banking system. These other banks are supervised by the relevant national agencies, though in a framework set by the supervisory arm of the ECB. Angeloni (2020, p. 39) explains how, often, 'there is little difference between banks belonging to different categories in terms of their size or type of business', adding that many 'are mid-sized and close to the significance asset threshold of €30 billion'. To avoid incompatibilities between supervisory regimes and rules governing resolution, he suggests closer harmonisation of rules applying to the banks supervised at the national level. How to treat the sovereign debt held by banks, hitherto regarded as safe (or 'normally' safe) assets, is tricky and will become more so in the aftermath of Covid-19.

The most politically sensitive issue around banking union is deposit insurance, seen from the earliest proposals as the necessary third leg alongside common supervision and resolution. The European Commission (2015b) put forward a proposal for a European Deposit Insurance Scheme (EDIS) to evolve through three phases: a reinsurance scheme, a co-insurance scheme and a full insurance scheme, implemented over a ten-year period. Since then, EDIS has been mired in linked disputes about, from one perspective, risk-sharing versus risk reduction, and, from another, moral hazard versus solidarity. Luis de Guindos, Vice-President of the ECB, bemoaned the lack of 'political will to implement this third pillar of the banking union'.[14] He added: 'so long as deposit insurance remains at the national level, the link between a bank and its home sovereign

---

[14] Speaking at a conference on 'Strengthening the EU's bank crisis management and deposit insurance framework: For a more resilient and efficient banking union', organised by the European Commission, 18 March 2021, http://bit.ly/3FeIV04.

persists'. Commenting on an attempt, in June 2021, to reach agreement, he said that it was 'not good news' that the latest attempt had again failed.[15]

The Single Resolution Fund (SRF) is only due to reach its intended target size by 2023; although discussions about a backstop for resolution have advanced, they are not yet settled. If the taxpayer is to be the ultimate guarantor of the banking system, even with quite onerous rules for how different classes of creditors incur the first tranches of losses, the fiscal capacity has to be commensurate with the possible scale of the bank loss. In 2008, the UK – just – coped with the sudden rescue of two of the country's biggest banks, although subsequent accounts by those involved (Darling, 2012) reveal just how fraught with both difficulty and danger it was to raise an amount comparable to the planned level of the SRF. Ireland, where the banking system was larger relative to GDP than in the UK, could not manage it, while the (botched) handling of the banking crisis in Cyprus highlighted the tricky political economy of rescue mechanisms.

An increasingly likely solution is to enable the ESM to be the fiscal backstop, but it is inhibited by the terms of the intergovernmental treaty through which it was established. It almost did so for Spain in 2012, but with the difference that the funding it provided was to the Spanish government, thereby maintaining the link between the national government and the banking sector, and avoiding a direct EU bailout of national banks. As in many other contexts, the objection from creditor countries is to assuming the burden of risk.

To some extent, the ECB's willingness to provide liquidity to the banking system has mitigated the problem in the short term, but with what some regard as uncomfortable consequences. In particular, by providing funds that ease the burden on national governments, the ECB is acting in a quasi-fiscal role and there are complex arguments about whether its actions mean that, for example, savers in fiscally more disciplined countries are effectively being penalised (through lower interest rates) to shore up more profligate governments. In a persuasive essay on 'helicopter money', Cecchetti and Schoenholtz (2016) explain why what central banks like the ECB have been doing by buying up public debt is, in practice, financing fiscal expansion rather than the traditional view attributed to Friedman of stoking inflation.

5.4 The Rocky and Contested Road to Fiscal Union

Running through much of the post-crisis debate on completing EMU is the vexed question of fiscal union, overlapping more recently with the advocacy by many leading figures of a much-enhanced role for fiscal policy in macroeconomic policy.

---

[15] www.omfif.org/2021/07/after-strategy-review-ecb-walks-inflation-tightrope/?utm_source= omfifupdate.

The difficulty with fiscal union is that there are very different conceptions of what it could entail (Bastian et al., 2011; Fuest and Piechl, 2012). Yet something going beyond current arrangements will be needed; its rationale has to make sense and the details of its design will matter. Much of the case for it turns on shortcomings in the toolkit for macroeconomic stabilisation which mean that national decisions on fiscal policy pay little heed to collective policy needs. Equally, fiscal union has to achieve a delicate compromise between, on the one hand, the stabilisation objective and, on the other, the distributive and allocative functions of fiscal policy. What makes sense for a complete EMU will be a mix of minimum 'necessary' conditions to enable an economic union to function and more far-reaching 'sufficient' conditions to ensure effective, and possibly also more legitimate, governance. The prevalence of austerity policies after the euro crisis made these fiscal dilemmas more acute because applying such policies simultaneously in several countries linked by close trading relationships caused negative spillover effects to amplify the resulting fall in demand (Alesina et al., 2019).

At least five distinct forms of fiscal union, each reflecting different political compromises and strategic visions of the euro, can be envisaged for the Eurozone (possibly for the EU as a whole), with differing mixes of risk reduction and risk-sharing.

- A first, comparatively narrow, variant is more intrusive oversight at the EU level of governance of national budgetary policies. The reforms embodied in the six-pack, the two-pack and the Fiscal Compact effectively moved the European Union (and, more so, the euro area) in this direction. Because the focus is fiscal discipline through adherence to rules, this form of fiscal union is manifestly about reducing risks. It became the direction of travel after the worst of the euro crisis and could be characterised as a German/Dutch preference, with support from other (mainly 'Northern') creditor members of the Eurozone.
- The second interpretation of fiscal union is the provision of support by either EU institutions or partner countries for governments encountering financing difficulties, resulting in higher interest rates and the prospect of insolvency. The bailouts for Greece (especially), Ireland, Portugal and Cyprus exemplify this approach, complemented by ECB bond purchases. The creation of the ESM was a means of sharing risk, but the fact that ESM loans require stringent conditions to be met also entails risk reduction.
- Some form of supranational stabilisation policy could be imagined as a third form of fiscal union. Rather than relying only on coordination of national policies to arrive at a common Eurozone fiscal stance, either an additional fiscal capacity could be introduced, or there could be ad hoc funds (e.g. an unemployment-related one) that provide a degree of

automatic stabilisation to counter asymmetric shocks. Here, too, there has been some movement, albeit not on a scale likely to make a huge difference, although the pandemic response could be crucial (see later).

- Risk-sharing would be enhanced if there were mutualisation, whether of public debt (some variant on Eurobonds) or more narrowly through common deposit insurance. In both cases, a collective fiscal backstop would be a logical complement to the existence of the mutualised risks. This fourth interpretation of fiscal union is, manifestly, strongly resisted by the net creditor countries, not least because of moral hazard arguments.
- Fifth, it could mean a system of transfers from Member States with relatively abundant public resources to fiscally strapped parts of the European Union to pay for public services (a genuine transfer union). This would mean redistributing resources permanently, rather than pure risk-sharing. Although such measures would also have a demand-stabilising effect, they seem a remote prospect, highlighting how far the EU would need to shift to arrive at a fiscal constitution comparable to those in place in other leading currency areas.

In addition to these macroeconomic conceptions, associated with how best to manage EMU, there could be moves towards harmonisation of taxes (for instance, on single market grounds), or harmonisation of a broader range of expenditure entitlements than at present. Although the pandemic gave a renewed impetus to economic coordination, opposition to common taxes remains strong.

A further governance change to the fiscal framework was the agreement by euro area members and the other EU signatories of the Fiscal Compact to establish independent fiscal councils (IFCs). Their primary functions are to monitor whether the public finances are in line with relevant rules and to assess the risks of deviation from these rules. The governance aim they fulfil is to increase the national 'ownership' of fiscal rules. The legislation did not specify the precise form that IFCs should take, and they do differ in their role markedly among the Member States. By 2021, only Poland did not have a body that can be convincingly identified as an IFC (Davoodi et al., 2022).

A ranking exercise by the European Commission[16] assesses the scope of the various national bodies according to a range of criteria, generating an index on a scale from 0 to 100. Implicitly, the higher the score, the more consequential the Council. Low scores are assessed for Croatia and, to a lesser extent, Finland and Sweden, whereas the highest scores are in Austria, Malta and Italy. It is hard to judge whether fiscal councils have lived up to the expectations vested in them, but in some countries they have provided a worthwhile addition to the policy framework.

---

[16] https://ec.europa.eu/info/publications/fiscal-institutions-database_en.

5.5 A Hamiltonian Moment? Not Quite . . .

The EU economic response to the Covid-19 crisis produced an agreement on a supranational fiscal response that could become a turning-point in EMU governance, but it also exposed deep resistance to a more comprehensive fiscal/political union. Potential borrowing directly from the markets by the supranational level for macroeconomic stabilisation purposes elicited strong feelings when France and Germany proposed a recovery fund. After difficult negotiations, the Next Generation EU (NGEU) package was agreed, with a mix of loans and direct grants, alongside the much-delayed agreement on the Multiannual Financial Framework (MFF) for 2021–7. Its great virtue in the midst of the pandemic was to avoid adding to the national debt burdens.

From the standpoint of completing EMU, it could break the deadlock on a number of key elements of the governance framework. Box 1 presents the principal features of the package. For Germany, this was a significant shift, although other 'Northern' countries were resistant, despite reassurances about the temporary nature of the package. Unsurprisingly, the more indebted Member States, notably Italy, strongly supported the idea.

There was much talk of a 'Hamiltonian'[17] moment, although it is important also to be clear on the nature of the 1790 moment in the United States. As several of the contributors to a 'symposium of views' published by *The International Economy*[18] attest, the crucial feature of Hamilton's plan was to mutualise state debts at the federal level, in effect creating the T-bond. Plainly, the new NGEU does not envisage the assumption of the *existing* debts of the Member States by the EU level. Instead, it enables the EU level to borrow in its own right to fund public spending. While alleviating the pressure on national public finances, it is qualitatively different from the borrowing previously undertaken by EU agencies (the European Investment Bank (EIB) and the ESM), both of which enable Member States to borrow on keener terms and for specific purposes. In effect, it is partly a Keynesian fiscal stimulus from the supranational level and, as such, does break new ground, but it is also partly a stream of funding for the EU's green deal and digital ambitions, with an element of cross-border transfers of public spending. It is not Hamiltonian, but, to employ a different metaphor, it is the crossing of a Rubicon.

A novel feature of the plan is how the borrowing will be repaid. The Commission proposed that it be over a thirty-year period 'not before 2028 and not after 2058' and an expectation was to create new EU 'own resources' for this purpose. An EU 'power to tax' has, however, been anathema for many

---

[17] The reference is to the 1790 decision by Alexander Hamilton, the First US Treasury Secretary.
[18] www.international-economy.com/TIE_Su20_EUHamiltonSymp.pdf.

Box 1 The next generation EU recovery package

The headline total amount of the package is €750 billion at 2018 prices, composed of grants worth €390 billion and loans for the balance of €360 billion. Initial proposals were for the balance to be two-thirds grants and one-third loans, but objections from net contributor countries reduced the grant component.

It is funded by borrowing by the European Commission directly from financial markets and is to be repaid no later than 2058, from revenue raised from new EU 'own resources'. It will be administered through EU budget mechanisms.

The bulk of the money is allocated to a new Recovery and Resilience Facility (89.7 per cent), with the rest going mainly to React-EU (6.3 per cent; a fund to top up existing Cohesion Policy commitments), rural development (1 per cent) and the EU's INVESTEU (0.8 per cent) and Horizon research programmes (0.7 per cent).

The allocations by Member State were based on a complex formula reflecting conditions both before and during the pandemic. The result is, broadly, to favour southern, central and eastern Europe, with net contributions from north-western Member States.

Recipients are expected to give priority to investment projects consistent with the EU's green deal and digitalisation aims and have to put forward comprehensive plans for how the money will be used. These have to be approved by, and will be monitored by, the European Commission, albeit with a much lighter touch than Cohesion Policy.

Formally, the package is a temporary measure with no provision for renewal or becoming a permanent instrument of governance.

Member States, but by agreeing to hypothecate future revenues to the repayment of the NGEU borrowing, a different dimension of 'Hamiltonian' may have been realised. Hamilton's proposition required federal taxes and, in this respect, the moment may be more significant than it appears. Attention has mainly focussed on whether the door has been opened to a borrowing capability, but an EU power to tax may prove to be more 'Hamiltonian'.

There is much speculation about whether EU support for Ukraine will necessitate a similar EU funding package and, by so doing, metamorphose into an acceptance of a substantially increased fiscal capacity. A difficulty in relation to legitimation is that the Parliament, which has clear powers on the spending side of the EU budget – though limited on the revenue side – has been somewhat sidelined in the manner in which new instruments have been decided and will be monitored. As Begg et al. (2022) show, the Parliament's involvement in NGEU and other borrowing instruments is qualitatively lower than for the MFF, and this worries its members.

6 The Findings of the Survey Are Revealing

The many insights garnered from the expert survey provide a mix of assessments on the state of play and the prospects for arriving at a complete and genuine EMU. For a list of those consulted, see Annex 1.

6.1 Membership of the Eurozone

Most respondents are clear that the euro is here to stay, with only 15 per cent of respondents answering 'possibly' on whether a break-up of the euro is to be expected by 2030, while 19 per cent said 'no chance' and 66 per cent thought it unlikely. Nearly four in five respondents expected the membership of the Eurozone to increase in the next decade, with only one envisaging a fall and the balance saying that it will stay the same. Bulgaria and Croatia, the latter already now set to join in 2023, were mentioned most often as the likeliest 'joiners'. For a handful of respondents, Italy is seen as a possible 'leaver', albeit with a low probability, and even among the few who fear for Italy's membership, most see exit as so damaging that it will be avoided.

Some respondents believe that Romania has strong political incentives to join soon, while Vivien Schmidt goes further, expecting several of the remaining central and eastern European countries to join because (in her words) 'increasing fears of Russian seeming aggression [are leading] them to seek a deeper embrace of the EU and its headline policy community, the Euro'. However, Michael Landesmann, a close observer of the Visegrad countries over many years, is doubtful about an accession by Romania in the next decade. Several respondents mention the possibility of Denmark, including Lorenzo Bini Smaghi, who also raises the tantalising prospect of Scotland joining.

Taking the evidence from the survey and other sources into account, full alignment between EU membership and full participation in EMU remains unlikely over the next decade, hence EMU will remain both incomplete in this respect and institutionally suboptimal. With Brexit removing the largest of the non-participating countries, in one survey respondent's words, 'the non-Eurozone part of the EU has lost a centre of gravity'. The upshot could see Poland becoming pivotal and, although its stance remains one of being wary about euro area membership, a change of government could shift its position.

Incomplete membership has ramifications. Erik Nielsen of Unicredit (with long experience of financial markets) believes that 'the eurozone needs to develop its own institutions and not remain dependent on non-EMU EU members and EU institutions'. Stefano Micossi of Assonime is forthright in linking financial integration and the number of full participants in EMU: 'Membership can increase only if sovereign debt overhang finds common solutions and stronger crisis management solutions to reassure investors and countries of a solid future for the euro.' An intriguing point made by Hrvoje Butkovic from Croatia concerns the absence of any mechanism for exiting the euro: 'Turning the Euro into a "Hotel California" whereby once the country enters it can never leave creates political problems and fuels Euroscepticism.'

6.2 Governance of the Euro

There are strong clusters of opinion about priorities for completing EMU – irrespective of political feasibility – summarised in Table 1. The strongest support, ranked as either 'vital' or 'useful', was for common deposit insurance and having a European level fiscal backstop, with only a handful of respondents seeing either as a low priority. Having a common safe asset was also strongly supported, although fully fledged Eurobonds were considered 'useful', rather than 'vital'.

A similar proportion favours having a European unemployment insurance scheme providing reinsurance for national schemes, but an EU scheme offering direct unemployment insurance obtained less support. This is not wholly surprising to the extent that reinsurance can be regarded much more as a stabilisation instrument, whereas direct insurance would stray into social policy. By contrast, there is little appetite for stricter fiscal rules, suggesting a significant shift away from the reactions to the sovereign debt crisis of the early 2010s, which saw so much emphasis on such rules.

Perhaps reflecting the initial (just before the survey was launched) agreement on the NGEU pandemic recovery package, establishing the principle of EU level borrowing to finance spending programmes, it is striking how much support there was among survey respondents for future EU borrowing, a Eurozone budget and taxes, and a Eurozone treasury. If these were to be realised, they would represent a significant deepening of EMU, while also opening up more of a gap between those participating in the euro and those outside. Although there is weak support for enhanced fiscal discretion, John Fitzgerald (Trinity College, Dublin) comments that 'a mechanism for co-ordinating the fiscal stance of the eurozone would be very beneficial – even if it is only a pipe dream'.

Several respondents closest to financial markets regard completion of banking union and capital markets union as the most pressing priorities. Erik Nielsen

Table 1 Priorities for completing EMU

Importance Potential innovation	VITAL	USEFUL	LOW PRIORITY	NOT AT ALL NEEDED	UNSURE	TOTAL
Common deposit insurance (EDIS)	45.87%	46.79%	6.42%	0.00%	0.92%	
	50	51	7	0	1	109
A European-level fiscal backstop	51.43%	40.95%	5.71%	0.00%	1.90%	
	54	43	6	0	2	105
A common safe asset	43.40%	42.45%	9.43%	1.89%	2.83%	
	46	45	10	2	3	106
Fully fledged Eurobonds	16.67%	56.48%	13.89%	6.48%	6.48%	
	18	61	15	7	7	108
A European unemployment scheme offering only reinsurance	11.21%	56.07%	21.50%	6.54%	4.67%	
	12	60	23	7	5	107
A European unemployment scheme offering direct payments to claimants	6.42%	33.94%	32.11%	22.94%	4.59%	
	7	37	35	25	5	109
A dedicated Eurozone budget	27.78%	43.52%	22.22%	4.63%	1.85%	
	30	47	24	5	2	108

Table 1 (cont.)

Importance Potential innovation	VITAL	USEFUL	LOW PRIORITY	NOT AT ALL NEEDED	UNSURE	TOTAL
Eurozone borrowing capacity	43.93% 47	38.32% 41	11.21% 12	5.61% 6	0.93% 1	107
A Eurozone finance minister	14.68% 16	44.95% 49	27.52% 30	11.93% 13	0.92% 1	109
A Eurozone Treasury	16.82% 18	48.60% 52	26.17% 28	7.48% 8	0.93% 1	107
Eurozone taxes	24.07% 26	40.74% 44	26.85% 29	5.56% 6	2.78% 3	108
Stricter fiscal rules	12.96% 14	15.74% 17	41.67% 45	26.85% 29	2.78% 3	108
More fiscal discretion for Member States	12.15% 13	22.43% 24	42.06% 45	19.63% 21	3.74% 4	107

explains the rationale: 'The private sector can play its role in cushioning asymmetric shocks as in other large currency unions.' In part, too, the financial dimension of union has to go faster because of worries about, as one respondent expressed it, the ECB being 'overburdened in the current context' and the euro area needing 'more equity financing and less debt'. To ease this pressure, John Springford of the Centre for European Reform believes that 'tax-raising, borrowing and spending at the EU/eurozone level will ultimately be necessary', but a practitioner who requested anonymity is sceptical: 'The willingness to do this does currently not seem to exist.'

More than 72 per cent of respondents would like to see the ESM integrated into the EU legal order, rather than remaining a separate intergovernmental treaty, with a further 16 per cent saying that it would make no difference and only a handful opposed. Whether it might become a European Monetary Fund, with a wider remit to support economic adjustment, or be available for all Member States remain open questions.

These are politically extremely delicate matters, but they highlight the awkwardness of having a large core of Eurozone countries inside a looser EU, yet a lack of agreement on interactions between the two levels. A parallel David Howarth (University of Luxembourg political scientist) draws with the IMF is that 'legitimacy and accountability problems for the ESM' need to be resolved. He cites the Italian government's opposition to the conditionality ESM support would have entailed had it sought pandemic-related loans. The views of political scientists are also instructive on aspects of a complete union too easily overlooked by economists and the financial world. For many, the democratic legitimacy and accountability dimension of completing EMU rarely goes much beyond warm words. But, as Kevin Featherstone (LSE) warns:

> The sustainability of the EZ requires much closer and more sensitive attention to fundamental features of governance. Here, political science perspectives on accountability, legitimacy, and support mechanisms for those states with poor quality institutions can be helpful – each tied to considerations of enabling a more diverse set of socio-economic models to develop according to domestic preferences. Crudely, the EZ must be seen to break out of the narrow ideologization of recent times, privileging one ordo-liberal inspired orthodoxy and constitutionalizing it so it becomes synonymous with the European ideal. The EU needs to reach out to those disaffected by this narrowness and exclusivity. The rise of eurosceptic populism is a direct result in a heterogenous union – Europe is 'othered', an antagonist to its weaker states.

Vivien Schmidt says that an economically genuine EMU 'won't succeed politically unless Member States have greater freedom to decide the what and how to "grow" their economies'. Uwe Puetter sees politicisation of some aspects of

EMU governance, such as the semester, as necessary: it should have 'fewer issues to look at, more Eurogroup and European Council attention for a small set of priorities'. Failure to accommodate legitimacy, says Anne-Laure Delatte, a CNRS expert on euro crises, will 'be used by populist parties against the European project', while Sonja Puntscher-Riekmann (Salzburg University) worries about 'the asymmetry between monetary and economic/fiscal/social policies'. Thomas Wieser, a prominent former Eurogroup official, issues a plea: 'There needs to be a more honest debate about the loss of sovereignty within a monetary union that goes far beyond monetary. Avoiding this is understandable, but naive and dangerous.'

6.3 Fiscal Rules

Unsurprisingly, as experts, the respondents are generally familiar with the SGP, but a striking proportion of them (55 per cent) adjudge it to have 'limited effect', with the balance split between those who consider it either 'fairly effective' or as 'having no effect'. For an instrument meant to be at the heart of Eurozone governance, this is a damning finding. Even so, 86 per cent of respondents believe that there is a need for some form of SGP. There are divided opinions on whether national rules would be a better option, as has been suggested in a number of recent contributions to the literature, with the great majority of respondents (63 per cent) opting for the answer 'depends on the context'.

6.3.1 The Stability and Growth Pact

The survey responses on the SGP and on fiscal rules reveal some differences between academics from economics backgrounds, on the one hand, and, on the other, political figures, legal scholars and academic political scientists. The latter devote far more attention to the political consequences and the implications for governance. Pervenche Beres, formerly chair of the European Parliament's ECON committee, recalls that there is a need 'to consider "economic policies as a matter of common concerns" but it should be more democratic, less complex, better shared and targeting the right objectives related to long[-]term investment and ecological transition'. She doubts the SGP 'could be the right basis to move in that direction'. Irish legal expert Imelda Maher observes that

> considered reform is usually necessary for many legal instruments as the environment within which they operate changes. Frequent reform can be indicative of poor law making and an attempt to use law to articulate ineffective and incomplete political compromises. The SGP relied too much on non-binding legal norms (soft law) which nonetheless were capable

of having legal effects. This has been much improved now. A clear articulation of learning from the new regime should first be set out before any reform.

Among economists the focus is more on the underlying economic rationale for rules and the variables to be targeted, though with some sharp differences of opinion. A cryptic comment from Jérôme Haegeli, of Swiss Re, is 'SGP="Stability and Growth Pact", but where is the Growth pact?', while Panos Tsakoglou, now in the Greek government, argues that 'it should be symmetric (not only for excessive deficits, but for excessive surpluses, too)'. Others feel that the SGP is too loose, but argue for a different configuration of rules; for example, Jakob De Haan of the Dutch central bank advocates 'less flexibility (no escape clauses) and focus on debt instead of deficit', while Stefano Micossi advocates 'a reformed SGP centred on a debt rule or expenditure rule' linked to debt sustainability.

Despite its shortcomings, the SGP has some merit: Holger Schmieding of Berenberg Bank asserts that 'even if SGP rules are often honoured in the breach, the dismal fiscal experience of the US and the UK shows that having no such rules, or changing them under every finance minister as in the UK, is far worse than the SGP'. Roel Beetsma, a Dutch academic and member of the European Fiscal Board (EFB), says: 'Obviously the SGP has not worked perfectly, but it has generated an equilibrium in which countries have contained budget deficits that would otherwise have been larger.' Two economic journalists stress the political function of EU fiscal rules: Martin Sandbu (*Financial Times*) justifies them 'more for political reasons than economic'; for David Smith of the *Sunday Times*, they remain a reassurance, particularly for the northern European countries.

For completing EMU, three main messages can be discerned. The first is the excessive complexity of the SGP and the damage this does to the credibility of the rules. Michele Chang (College of Europe) summarises: 'Too complex, too easy to ignore', while Zsolt Darvas of Bruegel suggests that overly complex rules 'hinder their internalisation by policymakers and their acceptance by the wider public'. He calls for 'a simple new rule: nominal expenditures should not grow faster than long-term nominal income, and they should grow at a slower pace in countries with excessive debt levels'.

Nevertheless, a second message is that a common framework is needed, albeit one that a respondent says encompasses a 'political governance scheme, not rule based governance'. Jean Pisani-Ferry acknowledges the 'need for a fiscal framework because there are significant fiscal externalities. But the Maastricht-based system of detailed numerical rules is dead.' Robert Skidelsky puts it succinctly: 'A fiscal constitution with escape clauses is needed in any case. The question is the nature of the constitution. The present system constrains desirable fiscal interventions.' For Jacques Le Cacheux (Université de Pau et des pays de l'Adour), 'some common rule for national fiscal policies is probably needed for the sake of mutual trust and for coordination'. Several of the holders of public office with a close interest in fiscal policy concur, as the following (unattributed, to respect their confidentiality) comments demonstrate:

- 'effective and credible fiscal coordination is a prerequisite for further steps towards fiscal union';
- 'monetary union requires a matching fiscal pillar, including a risk-free asset, policy coordination or a central decision-making body. In the absence of this centralized power, it is indispensable to have tight coordination of national fiscal policies';
- 'some form of fiscal coordination is needed, especially in the absence of a common eurozone fiscal policy, but the current SGP must be modified substantially to allow for more countercyclicality and more investment, and to take into account more international trade and the current account balance'.

Third, there is the vexed question of whether the SGP or other fiscal rules make a difference. Daniel Gros of CEPS damns the SGP with faint praise, saying that it is 'mostly a paper tiger, but useful to set some broad policy parameters'. Waltraud Schelkle (LSE) suggests that 'fiscal rules can be a forum for coordination and provide an anchor for discussions about the macroeconomic stance' of the euro area, but she adds: 'For disciplining individual countries, I do not expect much from the SGP.' French economist Olivier Marty suggests a need for 'a carrot and stick approach' because he worries about the damaging effects of 'renewed divergences (macro, social, political) and the impact they would have on Eurozone integrity'.

Certain directions for change are identified. Marco Buti, a leading Commission official, makes a connection between rules and deepening of EMU, arguing that 'there is a link between the establishment of a central fiscal capacity and the stringency of fiscal rules: the former requires the latter'. French journalist Sabine Syfuss-Arnaud observes that attitudes towards the SGP depend on whether 'you have a northern point of view or a southern one', something also apparent from the mix of responses to the survey. She suggests that it can be effective, 'but it is also a political dynamite that Berlin, and others like Austria or the Netherlands, have difficulties to handle (i.e. the drama of the men in black in Greece)'.

For Piotr Arak of the Polish Economic Institute, 'the problem is that within the same framework we have very different economies with legacy policies and debt which was incurred before and thanks to lower interest rates the debt levels increased. Some countries manage good and prudent policies but for some this did not work and probably it never will.' In the same vein, journalist Mathieu Solal says that 'imposing the same discipline and rigid figures on countries with such different budgetary and economical situations does not make sense'. Ramunas Vilpiskauskas of Vilnius University argues that 'the COVID-19 crisis has created a new context for the SGP rules and fiscal rules more generally, but the reality of limited resources will come back when the debts will have to be serviced'. Others would like to see a form of 'golden' rule, separating public investment from public consumption.

6.3.2 National Rules

Regarding what sort of national rule would be most useful, two-thirds consider that an expenditure rule – aimed at containing the level of public spending – is either useful or necessary. A debt rule – typically limiting the debt to GDP ratio and found already in several EU countries – is also considered necessary or useful. By contrast, two-thirds of respondents believe that a balanced budget rule – deterring fiscal deficits, as in most US states – would be of limited value or counterproductive. As Table 2 shows, marginally the greatest overall support, taking into account the 29 per cent regarding the option as 'necessary', was for a combination of rules.

However, Erik Jones (now heading the Robert Schuman Centre at the EUI) argues that 'the most effective rules are those that force some kind of reconciliation between spending and taxation and that require cross-party political cooperation'. Corrado Machiarelli (NIESR) stresses that 'what matters from the point of view of fiscal sustainability is the expenditure's composition', notably how much productive investment there is. In the same vein, Clemens Fuest (President of IFO) offers concise advice: 'We do not need stricter but smarter fiscal rules. We also need more credible debt restructuring mechanisms. To achieve that we need a combination of more solidarity and more market discipline.'

6.4 The Semester

In view of the widespread criticisms of the effectiveness of EU monitoring on national governments, there is surprisingly strong support for the European semester, with 70 per cent of respondents adjudging it to be a worthwhile instrument of governance, against 18 per cent saying that it is not. On whether it is needed at all, Andy Watt of Hans Böckler Stiftung answers 'yes, but', going on to comment that it does 'not really play a strong coordinating role where it is needed (beyond some peer pressure) and creates a lot of bitterness and criticism of EU "interference" and non-respect of national democracy'.

Table 2 Preferences for national fiscal rules

Preference Type of rule	NECESSARY	CAN BE USEFUL	LIMITED VALUE	COUNTER-PRODUCTIVE	TOTAL
Balanced budget	2.27%	29.55%	26.14%	42.05%	
	2	26	23	37	88
Expenditure ceiling	19.57%	47.83%	15.22%	17.39%	
	18	44	14	16	92
Debt to GDP ratio ceiling	10.87%	45.65%	28.26%	15.22%	
	10	42	26	14	92
A combination of some or all of the above	29.03%	45.16%	10.75%	15.05%	
	27	42	10	14	93

John Fitzgerald would like there to be a sharper 'focus on co-ordinating the euro area fiscal stance'.

However, practitioners are more positive, with one respondent regarding it as 'a very useful process of centralized assessment and peer review', though it would benefit from 'a deeper analysis of economic relations between the different Member States'. François Villeroy de Galhau (Gouverneur of the Banque de France) considers it 'a worthwhile instrument to ensure coordination of national economic policies', but would like 'to complement it with further common initiatives and to define a proper policy-mix to support a collective economic strategy'. Marco Buti says that, with the advent of new funding from NGEU, 'financial incentives associated to packages of reforms and investments will make coordination much more meaningful', a point echoed by former European Commissioner Joaquin Almunia, while Italian economist Lorenzo Codogno believes that 'the current shift toward a structure of incentives instead of punishments is probably the right one'.

A repeated criticism is that it lacks teeth (for example, from Bert Kuby of the Committee of the Regions, who also argues that it needs 'more ownership by all actors'), leading Panicos Demetriades from the University of Leicester to advocate 'giving more powers to the European Commission to ensure members states follow any recommendations from this process', though he adds: 'but this is unlikely'. Thomas Wieser observes that 'there has never been an attempt to increase the political costs of not following recommendations'. David Howarth also notes 'a great deal of scepticism' about the indicators used, coupled with weak follow-up at the 'national level by governments responding to country recommendations', while Charles Wyplosz suggests the perverse effect that 'pressure from "Brussels" only feeds anti-Europe sentiment'.

For several respondents, the semester has lost its way: Robert Holzmann (Governor of the Austrian Central Bank) says that 'it had some value at the beginning but seems to have lost most of its effectiveness in the meantime'. Former Greek Finance Minister George Papaconstantinou says that 'a more effective semester will have to involve institutional steps to make it operational' and David Cameron of Yale University says that it needs to be 'upgraded, with more time for careful scrutiny'. According to former European Commissioner Laszlo Andor, 'it only makes sense if it is linked to a long-term strategy of economic and social development, like Europe 2020', implying that 'reviving the long-term approach would help the Semester'. Marjan Svetlicic (University of Ljubljana) is one of a number of commentators to assert that 'big and small countries are sometimes not equally treated. There are sometimes stereotypes about the Southern or new members, even applying harsher policies on them.' He suggests that this was the case for Slovenia.

6.5 The European Fiscal Board

More than 70 per cent of respondents are familiar or broadly familiar with what the EFB does – only 9 per cent do not know – and it is evaluated favourably by many. Francois Villeroy de Galhau argues that 'the role of the board is indeed crucial to have an independent opinion on fiscal stance, both at the national and at the EU level. Within its mandate the board has made valuable proposals that could be taken into account to improve the EU fiscal framework.' Andy Watt says that it has 'written some good reports', while Jean Pisani-Ferry maintains that 'it is doing good work'. David Howarth elaborates, calling the Board a 'group of respected experts' that 'provides real value-added, especially because these assessments come with less "political baggage" than those produced by the Eurogroup / Commission'.

However, Charles Wyplosz is more dismissive and reflects several other opinions: 'nice and good people talking to no one that matters. It must be separated from the Commission, adequately staffed and given oversight of national fiscal councils and the European budget', and Massimo Bordignon (one of its members) writes: 'We could have done much more had we had more resources and a more clear role in the Eurozone framework.' Jagjit Chadha (Director of NIESR) finds that it 'has had very little traction. It is mostly descriptive and needs to adopt more teeth to enhance its open mouth', while Vicky Pryce (Centre for Economic and Business Research) is dubious about 'whether changes take place as [a] result of its reports'.

Other comments also question the position and mandate of the EFB, and its influence on fiscal decision-making. Martin Sandbu would favour 'a more explicit and powerful function for setting the aggregate eurozone fiscal stance'. Former Italian Finance Minister Pier Carlo Padoan would like to see 'closer interaction with the Commission in drafting recommendations, while preserv-ing independence'. Holger Schmieding considers its role to be 'not strong enough[;] it is not independent enough. It falls short of a genuinely independent fiscal council', and Otmar Issing regrets that 'the idea of an independent FB was spoiled by the Commission taking control'. Karlis Bukovskis of the Latvian Institute for International Affairs echoes the sentiment: 'The idea of the European Fiscal Board was destroyed by the European Commission when it was made [] an appendix to the European Commission.'

Its visibility is open to challenge. For Amy Verdun (University of Victoria, Canada), 'the Board does not yet seem to be fully on the radar of many people. I think it may want to reach out a bit more to members in the policy community, academics, journalists, and clarify what it does. It may be still a bit esoteric to the uninitiated.' Sonja Puntscher-Riekmann similarly notes that the 'Board is unknown in public[;] its assessments need greater transparency as for criteria of judgment and visibility to gain legitimacy'. Some doubts about the independence of the Board are expressed forcibly by a number of respondents who asked not to be quoted directly: 'needs more administrative and functional autonomy'; could be 'made institutionally more independent and provided with more own resources'; 'should be more independent without relying on the Commission services'; and if the 'Fiscal Board deviates from Commission and governments, there should be "comply and explain" by the latter two'.

To render it more effective, several suggestions are made, with David Marsh calling for a 'bigger budget, stronger powers, wider competence'. Lars Jonung, who chaired the Swedish Fiscal Council, believes that the recommendations of the Board should be used more frequently by the Commission, while Angelo Martelli of LSE would like it to be 'more involved in the MIP decisions'. Joaquin Almunia adds a plea for 'a more transparent interaction with the national fiscal boards'. This tack is also pushed by Lorenzo Bini Smaghi for whom 'the responsibility for fiscal policy is ultimately political. The Fiscal Board can enhance accountability', while Laszlo Andor believes an enhanced role for the Board 'should form part of broader EMU reform, together with the Eurogroup which lacks transparency and democratic control'. Zsolt Darvas goes much further, suggesting that

> it should be changed to a European Fiscal Council (EUFC) . . . similar to the ECB's Governing Council: about six executive board members (with the same appointment and accountability procedures as for ECB executive members), plus the heads of national fiscal councils . . . with a focus on gross errors and cross-border spillovers'. He would not like its decisions to be binding, but they should 'be made public in a timely manner, providing a major input into the Commission's recommendations to the Council.

A key political difficulty is, however, highlighted by Thomas Wieser:

> the Commission fears that the EFB could [itself pronounce] on the opening (or not) of individual steps within the SGP procedure which would reveal the Commission to have politicised the whole process significantly. If that were changed the EFB (which is doing a great job) would become even more effective. Its independence from the Commission machinery would need to be increased.

6.6 Macroeconomic Imbalances Procedure

The respondents are mostly aware of the MIP – 89 per cent know what it does – but they were unimpressed with it. The median answer on its effectiveness was 'somewhat ineffective' with an even split between this and the answers 'somewhat effective' and 'ineffective', and no support for it being 'effective'. Even so, 62 per cent believe that it should be maintained and only 11 per cent said that it should not. Thomas Wieser calls it 'a useful signalling device, but nothing else', while Vicky Pryce notes that it is 'important to keep an eye on countries with high debt levels, high non-performing loans and low growth', but is sceptical about its ability to change national behaviour.

Clemens Fuest also regards it as 'useful because it encourages debate and policy coordination but its impact is limited', while Lars Jonung offers: 'Any dialogue is better than no dialogue.' Lorenzo Bini Smaghi wants the MIP to 'be more effective, more selective. It is in the interest of the EZ that imbalances are reduced.' For *Economist* journalist John Peet (and others) 'the big problem is that there is no sanction or even blame for the big surplus countries, Germany and the Netherlands. By putting adjustment on deficit countries, this gives the euro a deflationary bias.'

French economist Agnès Bénassy speaks for many others in saying that it 'needs to be reformed' . David Howarth would forgo sanctions: 'Peer pressure combined with sound analysis should be the limits of EU-level macroeconomic policy coordination.' Some, however, would prefer to consign it to history: Charles Wyplosz is trenchant, castigating the MIP as 'a useless exercise'. According to Jean Pisani-Ferry, 'it was a good move in principle but there is no point in keeping a procedure that has no teeth', and Peter Wostner of the Slovenian government is dubious about the 'value added of discussions . . . and the traffic light system', used to assess risks.

6.7 An Enhanced International Role for the Euro

Support for an enhanced international role for the euro was strikingly high with 86 per cent of respondents in favour and only 9 per cent against. These responses partly reflect the timing of the survey towards the end of the Trump Presidency, during which concerns about weaponization of the dollar were acute. There is much more ambivalence about whether greater internationalisation will happen in the next decade. Those who believe that it will (42 per cent) outnumber those who said 'no' by more than four to one, but a higher number (47 per cent) answered that it will depend on others.

Differing rationales for a more internationalised euro are put forward, with many respondents alluding to the benefits enjoyed by the United States from having the dominant global currency. François Villeroy de Galhau offers a compelling view: 'The euro must grow in importance internationally; primarily for obvious geopolitical reasons of European sovereignty. The US dollar is a clear advantage in the exercise of American power, while China is now concerned with the internationalisation of the renminbi.' Another public office holder identifies 'monetary sovereignty as key for financial stability and fiscal policy autonomy. If geopolitical tensions continue, there will likely be changes in the international monetary system, opening an opportunity to the euro to reinforce its role in the world.' Robert Holzmann asserts that an 'international role promises a number of relevant advantages at reasonable costs (e.g. liquidity provisioning), but progress will be limited'.

There are differing views on how actively internationalisation should be pursued. Thus, Nicolas Veron of the Peterson Institute for International Economics (PIIE) stresses that 'currency internationalization is always a market-driven process' and Otmar Issing, while adjudging internationalisation to be 'desirable, yes', says that it has to be 'based on internal stability and as the consequence of a demand[-]driven process'. Howard Davies, who chairs the Natwest banking group, is firm: 'If it happens, fine, but it should not be an explicit policy objective.' Perhaps optimistically, Lorenzo Bini Smaghi says: 'If there is no euro crisis in the coming decade, the international role of the euro will rise steadily.' Danae Kyriakopoulou, at the time chief economist of the OMFIF think-tank, stresses the euro's 'increased international role in the emerging field of green finance. The euro is the dominant currency in terms of green bond issuance, with almost half of green bonds issued in euros. This is a promising area for the internationalisation of the euro given the alignment with European strategies for a green transition.'

How can internationalisation of the euro be advanced? First, as has been said previously by Buti (2020), several respondents emphasise the need for the EU to complete the various reforms to strengthen the governance of the euro for internationalisation to advance. Necessary conditions, as Pier Carlo Padoan says, include 'completion of banking union and capital markets union', a point echoed by Marco Buti, who suggests that deepening of EMU also has to encompass fiscal union. More generally, as argued by David Marsh, 'this will only happen if there is more coherence and plausibility to the euro's own internal structures'. Several respondents highlight the need for a safe asset, but in this and related respects Stefano Micossi thinks 'the reluctance of Germany [will be the] main obstacle'.

Second, a clear connection is mooted by several respondents between the new borrowing to fund the EU recovery plan and the scope for internationalisation, precisely because it will create a larger market for euro-denominated securities without a national label. From a financial markets perspective, Reza Moghadam of Morgan Stanley believes: 'The Recovery Fund, by creating a large quantity of euro safe assets, enhances the attractiveness of holding euros by reserve managers.' According to Frank Vandenbroucke, now a minister in the Belgian government, 'the Recovery Fund initiative and the associated loans [should] lead to a more important role for the euro'. However, Michael Landesmann suspects that even 'with the issuing of bonds during the Covid-19 crisis', internationalisation 'will be rather slow and timid'.

The third is geopolitical developments and their impact on market sentiment. Jerry Cohen, despite his past scepticism, observes that 'an international euro would serve to protect and defend Europe's interests'. Cohen adds: 'As the dominance of the US dollar gradually fades, the euro is bound to receive more attention.' An interesting observation from Jean Pisani-Ferry is that 'the global context has changed significantly. It is time for the EU to have a view on developing the international role of the euro', but it should be 'for geopolitical rather than economic reasons'. However, François Villeroy de Galhau is one of several respondents who believe that 'there are also economic reasons: as globalisation has expanded over the past 20 years, wider use of the euro would help to protect our businesses against foreign exchange risks or legal disputes abroad. The concrete measures to promote the euro identified by the European Commission in December 2018 are therefore timely.'

The changing attitude of the United States is highlighted repeatedly by respondents: for Charles Wyplosz, 'if the dollar is becoming an instrument of foreign policy for the US, we need an alternative'. Panicos Demetriades says: 'Europe cannot afford to sit back while the US dollar dominates international transactions, especially if the USA has temperamental leaders like Donald Trump. No bank in Europe is safe from failure if the US authorities invoke the Patriot Act to prevent it from transacting in dollars.' Among others, György Szapáry of the Hungarian central bank regards the 'tendency by the US to weaponize the dollar' as a motivation for Europe. Loukas Tsoukalis highlights 'our collective vulnerability to unilateral decisions and sanctions made possible by the dominant role of the US dollar in the international financial system'.

Sahoko Kaji of Keio University adds that 'an increased international role for not just the euro but the EU helps other nations caught between the increasing animosity between China and the USA'. She has argued elsewhere (Kaji, 2020, p. 514) that Europe should develop a single payments app as a means of boosting the euro. In her view, such a development could 'help Europe become a soft and sharp global superpower with sensitivity, strong in consumer protection, leading in the field of advanced technology'. François Villeroy de Galhau also mentions payments systems: 'The development of fully unified European instant payment systems and integrated capital markets, and the later creation of a secure and broad euro-denominated security, would contribute to both the international expansion of the euro as well as its domestic consolidation.'

Former Greek Finance Minister Nicos Christodoulakis is representative of those who see the United States losing ground: 'The US gradual withdrawal from global affairs creates both the room and incentives for more EU involvement', while Jérôme Haegeli warns that the 'RMB is more likely to play an increased role in the international payment system than' the euro. But John Llewellyn, formerly Organisation for Economic Co-operation and Development (OECD) chief economist, demurs: 'China is making arguably negative progress with internationalising the renminbi, mainly because its government is less trusted than it was a few years ago.' Cinzia Alcidi sums up well:

> [Internationalisation] is politically desirable, as part of the EU search for strategic autonomy. Economic desirability is far less clear. Increasing the status of the euro as an international currency is not something that can be controlled politically. In a globalised world, this goes well beyond the use of a currency as reserve. Global trade invoicing and financial transactions are even more important, and there the role of the euro is very small.

6.8 Next Generation EU

Several respondents refer implicitly to how the game has changed because of the agreement on NGEU. For example, Paul de Grauwe (replying to the survey in early August 2020) says, with respect to the question of deepening the EMU, which he now regards as likely: 'Two months ago I would have chosen "unlikely", but with the Corona-pandemic so much more has become possible.' Corrado Machiarelli expresses fears about the continuing 'strong North–South divide' visible during the negotiations. Nevertheless, two-thirds of respondents believe that NGEU will lead to a permanent EU borrowing capacity, just 7 per cent believe that it will be temporary, and one practitioner observes that, even if temporary, it is an 'instrument to be used again in case of need'. François Villeroy de Galhau leans towards the view that it is 'an economic quantum leap toward a genuine common fiscal stabilisation tool', while John Peet says that 'it is a breakthrough, even if not a Hamiltonian moment. It will lead to some eurozone fiscal capacity and probably moves towards a safe asset and partial debt mutualisation.' French banker Bertrand Badré concurs: 'The Covid crisis has allowed a first move. Some have said it was an Hamiltonian moment. Not there yet. But Germany has moved. And this hopefully opens the doors to more to come. Both at EZ and EU level.'

Randall Henning of the American University applauds it as a 'conceptual breakthrough' but argues that its scope to become 'a more sustained counter-cyclical fiscal' mechanism will depend on the politics among Eurozone members. Mathieu Solal cautions that 'a lot will depend on the efficiency of this common effort', while Martin Weale, a former member of the Bank of England monetary policy committee, suspects that 'Germany will want to row back from allowing direct borrowing in more normal times. But they will probably not row back all the way.' The likely demands on the EU to support Ukraine economically once military action abates will reopen these questions.

But there is also a sense that the time-honoured EU approach of procrastination and incomplete solutions has to be confronted, even though one seasoned Brussels hand demurs: Daniel Gros believes that 'muddling through remains the most likely scenario'. Jonathan Portes of Kings College London pinpoints the challenge: 'The longer-term implications of the Next Generation EU fund are unclear but the logic will be additional deepening (at the EU or euro level).' An intriguing point made by Niku Määtänen (University of Helsinki) is that 'more fiscal risk-sharing and joint borrowing at the EU level ... diminishes the need for similar arrangements at the Eurozone level'.

7 Unfinished Business

'Listen carefully, and you can hear the creaking sound of the eurozone's tectonic plates tensing against one another. When such tensions are released, they can cause destruction. But they can also move mountains and reshape continents.'
– Martin Sandbu, *Financial Times,* 31 December 2019

The history of many existing federations shows that step changes towards fiscal union have occurred in response to 'exceptional events, often downturns in economic activity during deep crises' (Bordo et al., 2011, p. 24). Although the extent to which the EMU framework governance has changed is not always sufficiently appreciated, whether by market actors, or some policymakers and academic commentators, it is difficult to assess because so many of the new mechanisms have had protracted bedding-in periods. With the economic disruption from the invasion of Ukraine following hard on the heels of the pandemic, many are yet to be properly tested. For example, at the time of writing (autumn-2022) the SRF had not yet been called upon.

The agenda laid out in the *Four Presidents' Report* (European Council, 2012b), described earlier, provides a broad outline for a 'genuine', 'complete' or, to borrow a phrase from Papademos (2014), 'more perfect' EMU. How close is it? In rendering a verdict, several factors have to be taken into account. The first is whether enough has already been done to make the euro 'durable', even if it remains short of 'optimal', as a currency area. A second is whether, among the further reforms under discussion, enough are likely to be adopted. In spite of some of the changes that have given greater executive powers to EU- or Eurozone-level agencies and institutions, the governance model that has emerged is still far from being federal and, precisely for this reason, is bound to be more complex than one in which there is a clear intergovernmental division of powers and competencies.

A fundamental unresolved question is what role should be assigned to genuinely supranational bodies in EU, and especially Eurozone, economic governance. In significant respects, the reforms of recent years have taken powers away from elected national governments. They are now subject to more binding rules, more intrusive surveillance and more credible sanctions. Yet some commentators observe that although the European Commission has had its role as a watchdog strengthened, it has had little involvement in much of the key decision-making and that the crisis years have seen an extension of the role of national governments at the expense of the EU institutions. According to Puetter (2012) and subsequent analysis by Bickerton et al. (2015), dealing with the crisis brought the European Council to the fore in economic governance, where it has stayed, playing the dominant role in developing NGEU (Wessels et al., 2022).

Part of the problem, Pisani-Ferry (2014) contends, is that there are few voices speaking for the common interest, as opposed to those of individual Member States. The European Parliament has been tangential, while both the Commission and the ECB were confined to relatively limited roles, leaving only the Germans able to lead in this respect, and then only when the crisis was at a tipping-point at which there was no alternative but to act. Is there now any prospect of change?

Research conducted by the *EMUChoices* project finds that the period from after the sovereign debt crisis abated, up to the beginning of 2019, was not conducive to radical reform, with only a gradualist approach possible, according to a policy brief authored by Zdenek Kudrna.[19] This is explained by there being so little common ground between 'North' and 'South' coalitions on the direction of key reforms, but also by the limited scope for associating EMU reform with other bargains. As explained in the policy brief, 'deep divisions between the two coalitions, the single-dimensionality of the policy conflict and political backlash against technocratic policy-making impose severe constraints on the political feasibility of EMU reform proposals'. Two prescient findings from the *EMUChoices* project are worth citing. The first is that Franco-German cooperation could accelerate reform, not least because the two countries are leaders in the respective coalitions. Second, a 'crucial assumption of the gradualist scenario is that the E(M)U will be able to avoid existential crisis for a sufficiently long time to complete its reforms. While there is no reason to assume another global crisis in near future, it can never be excluded entirely.' Plainly, the pandemic is a new global crisis of rare ferocity and Ukraine is another.

---

[19] https://emuchoices.eu/wp-content/uploads/2019/05/PolicyBriedNo3.pdf.

7.1 The State of Play

As EMU is an amalgamation of different forms of union and there are differing degrees of completeness in each of these, any appraisal of them has to look not just at the appropriateness of technical solutions but also at whether they are likely to be politically acceptable. In this context, acceptability has to include the likely response of new governments, such as that of Giorgia Meloni in Italy. In addition, the normative dimension to the policy model at the heart of EMU cannot be ignored. Before considering what more is needed, Table 3 presents a summary of how complete the euro is as a currency.

Summing up, while the euro is closer to being a complete currency, mostly so in regard to monetary policy and banking union, it still falls short on all dimensions. By contrast, legitimation remains highly unsatisfactory. This should not be a surprise because the evolution of EMU is characterised by a proliferation of paradoxes. Thus, according to Wallace (2016, p. 267), 'in one of the many paradoxes of the euro experiment, the single currency that was once supposed to boost growth now itself needed growth if it was to continue in the long run'. He goes on to observe that 'another paradox in the story of the euro's survival was the fact that Germany had done particularly well despite all the angst about the rescue packages'.

Schelkle (2018, p. 2), pondering why the Eurozone has struggled to adopt effective mechanisms of risk-sharing, identifies 'the paradox that the more diverse potential members are, the larger the potential economic gains from monetary union, yet the more difficult it may be to realize these gains politically'. Among her explanations is the continuing mistrust between its members about free-riding and moral hazard. Fabbrini (2016) points, first, to the increased centralisation of oversight of fiscal policy in a system designed to give Member States budgetary autonomy, an outcome he adjudges to be more centralising than in the United States. Second, Fabbrini finds a paradox in what he calls the 'judicialization' of economic policymaking in which national courts and the ECB intervene in ways considered anathema in the United States. He notes a third paradox in the subversion of a system designed to give disproportionate voice to smaller states towards leadership by larger states.

7.2 A Further Reform?

'Believing in progress does not mean that any progress has yet been made.'

– Franz Kafka

Efforts to give a new impetus to completing EMU continued after the dust settled on the third Greek bailout crisis. But, partly because of the absence of any immediate crisis, there was little appetite for advancing some of the more

Table 3 Dimensions of a 'complete' currency: The euro assessed

Dimension	State of play	Prospects in next decade
Membership	19 out of 27	Could reach 22, possibly more
Monetary policy	ECB role has broadened to become a 'more normal' central bank	A further review of monetary policy strategy, but limited change
Banking union	Supervision and resolution mechanisms implemented, but common deposit insurance and EU level fiscal backstop still undecided	Reinsurance of deposits and backstop probable; continuing reluctance to move to common deposit insurance
Fiscal union	Bailout fund (ESM) agreed as intergovernmental mechanism; EU fiscal capacity at modest level, but changed by agreement of 'NGEU' measures	Prospect of EU-level borrowing becoming permanent feature; search for new approach to fiscal framework
Democratic legitimation	Little progress	Political pressures for greater accountability, but resistance from Member States
Other facets of governance	Value of semester, fiscal rules and MIP all questioned	Likely demands for greater scrutiny of governance procedures; potential capital markets union; centrality of climate change to policy
Internationalisation	Initial spurt after launch of euro, but little advance in last decade; second globally, but lagging well behind the US dollar	Expected to gain from doubts about the US dollar, offset by potential of renminbi; new momentum from market for European bonds to fund pandemic recovery

contentious dossiers in the *Five Presidents' Report*. The election of Emmanuel Macron as French President led to some speculation about a grand bargain with Germany in which the latter would consent to a deepening of EMU in return for an intensification of economic reforms in France.

Emmanuel Macron's 'Sorbonne' speech, delivered in September 2017, set out a powerful vision for deepening EMU, but gained little traction in many other capitals. His proposition was to confront the governance shortcomings in the right way *'si l'euro a vocation à devenir la monnaie de tous les Etats de l'Union lorsqu'ils remplissent les critères, construisons sans tarder une zone euro forte, efficace, solidaire et cette puissance bénéficiera demain à tous ceux qui la rejoindront'* [if the euro aspires to become the currency for all Member States of the Union once they fulfil the criteria, let us build, without delay, a strong effective and solidaristic euro and this strength will, in due course, help all who join it]. He also called for structural reforms at the national level to be complemented by 'une coordination de nos politiques économiques et un budget commun' [coordination of economic policies and a common budget] and for stronger political oversight, going on to emphasise how a strong and internationalised currency could enhance Europe as a global economic power.

Even as late as early March 2020, with Covid-19 spreading, the chances of progress on an EU fiscal capacity looked slender and, as one senior official explained, the difficult negotiations then underway on the EU's next MFF looked to have precluded a different approach for the duration of the MFF.[20] Nevertheless, in early February 2020, the Commission published a review of economic governance (European Commission, 2020), noting that 'the start of a new political cycle in the Union is an opportune and appropriate moment to assess the effectiveness of the current framework for economic and fiscal surveillance'. It recognised diverse shortcomings in the fiscal framework for EMU as a whole, as well as at the national level. Among these were:

- the tendency for fiscal policy to be pro-cyclical;
- too great an emphasis on current spending, often at the expense of public investment;
- the excessive complexity of the fiscal framework and the proliferation of rules, a consequence of which is too great a scope for non-compliance;
- a lack of symmetry in how macroeconomic imbalances are deterred, weighing mainly on deficit countries, but doing too little to deter excessive surpluses;

---

[20] Interview, Brussels, 28.02.2020.

- not enough attention to longer-term influences on fiscal sustainability, encapsulated in grand challenges around the environment, ageing and digital transformations.

The review therefore set three goals for a reformed system of EMU governance:

- sustainability of both growth performance and public finances and the avoidance of macroeconomic imbalances;
- a framework for policy surveillance able to facilitate closer policy coordination, especially in the euro area;
- promotion of convergence in economic performance.

The timing of its launch could scarcely be worse, barely days before the debilitating economic impact of Covid-19 become apparent, and it took until November 2022 for the European Commission (2022a) to publish its proposals. Their main thrust is to focus on medium term debt sustainability, rather than annual indicators, and to recognize national differences in fiscal risks. An assessment by Blanchard et al. (2022) is broadly positive, applauding the 'far-reaching' nature of the proposed changes, in contrast to previous reforms. They nevertheless point to shortcomings they believe need attention. Wyplosz (2022a) is more sceptical, arguing that while the two big ideas make sense, other proposals regarding sanctions and the extent of Commission involvement in the process are misguided.

In addition, there is the politically charged question of divergence in economic performance. As one respondent to the survey put it, if neglected, divergence could mean that 'the economic cost to the North will rise (fiscal transfers and monetary policy geared towards the South) as the divergence deepens. The situation is dynamically unstable.' Another respondent emphasises the limits of 'political acceptance in net payer countries'.

The proposals include only limited plans for new funding. Yet the European Fiscal Board (2020) underlined 'the difficulties of managing large shocks with hardly any joint elements, most importantly without the EU having a central fiscal capacity allowing it to borrow a meaningful amount of funds on the market'. While welcoming the temporary measures aimed at mitigating the crisis, the EFB argues that these provisional instruments 'should eventually be replaced by or morph into a permanent EU fiscal instrument so the EU can respond to severe shocks in a timely fashion'.

7.3 The Messy Politics of Further Reform

The lack of political consensus on a deeper fiscal union and starkly differing national preferences are daunting political barriers to such a change.

Creditor countries fret about the costs – both economic and, perhaps more so, political – they might incur if they take action to shore up struggling partner countries. There are also well-rehearsed formulae to defend the size and persistence of the surpluses on the current account of the balance of payments of these same creditor countries, and to counter the policy prescription that an expansion of (notably, German) domestic demand would go a long way towards curbing imbalances in the Eurozone.

The advent of a so-called New Hanseatic League comprising eight northern countries (the Netherlands, the three Nordic countries, the three Baltic countries and Ireland) constitutes a different grouping from the traditional North–South dichotomy. Most obviously, it has not explicitly been supported by Germany, despite being, arguably, in the latter's shadow. Rather, Germany has found itself torn between its normative support for the economic philosophy of the Hanseatics and its political need to work with France as the de facto leaders of the Eurozone.

Reform is also hampered by the provisions of the various EU treaties, bearing in mind that extensive Treaty change is a complex undertaking. Among the plethora of proposals for reform to enable EMU to function better, those of Maduro et al. (2021), bringing together legal and economic analyses, offer some plausible solutions that avoid the need for Treaty change. They suggest reinterpretation of the existing Treaty provisions to ease the constraints on the ECB in relation to unconventional monetary policy, building on NGEU, and identify two directions for an EU-level fiscal capacity: stabilisation or financing a higher volume of EU public goods. While NGEU does both, it is formally temporary. Rebecca Christie of the *Bruegel* think-tank, commenting on the successful roll-out of NGEU and the positive way it has been received by financial markets, but also noting the likely demands on the EU from the Ukraine crisis, observes that 'it would be a mistake to turn off the EU's public financing powers just when they came into their own'.[21]

But resistance has to be expected. A group, including a former SPD finance minister, a former European Commissioner and a former Minister-President of Bavaria, issued a call in the *Süddeutsche Zeitung* for a return to pre-crisis monetary orthodoxy: 'To make the euro area sustainable, a functioning, rules-based, controllable and enforceable set of rules is necessary, enforceable with penalties.' Writing before the surge in prices in 2022, the group pointed to risks from inflation and the adverse effects of persistently loose monetary policy. It called on the German government to restore fiscal discipline domestically, to

---

[21] OECD Forum Network, 'The European renewal: Making the most of pandemic recovery', http://bit.ly/3gSZrcH.

demand acceleration of economic reforms in other Eurozone countries and to push for revised but still binding Eurozone fiscal rules to be implemented. The group also said that it expects the ECB 'to return to its core task' of focussing on price stability and to rein in its bond purchases. The worry for other Member States is that the upshot could be a difficult battle over both future monetary policy strategy and the future EU fiscal framework.

7.4 Rethinking Fiscal Governance

While there are promising orientations in the November 2022 proposals for a new approach to the EU fiscal framework, the scope for fiscal policy to play a greater role remains constrained. There are two distinct strands to calls for greater use of fiscal policy for stabilisation purposes in EMU: revisiting the role of the national level; and establishing 'genuine' supranational capacities. Pre-pandemic, the national dimension had been constrained for three main reasons. First, the conjunction of the various EU and national rules had limited room for manoeuvre. Second, those with 'fiscal space', in the sense of debt and deficit parameters allowing a fiscal relaxation, have been unwilling to use it, while those with the most need for fiscal stimulus have lacked fiscal space: a classic Catch-22. The third, less discussed, reason is that economies close to full employment may be unable to absorb a fiscal expansion. Pre-pandemic, Germany arguably exemplified the third of these.

A paper starting from the pandemic-related suspension of EU fiscal rules (Blanchard et al., 2021, p. 2) suggested the EU fiscal framework has to find new answers to interrelated dimensions of 'fiscal Europe' when there is a return to a 'normal' characterised by much higher public debt. A first is the extent of fiscal union, defined to include mechanisms for 'increased risk sharing, common borrowing, and the size and use of the common EU budget'. In addition, a new approach to fiscal rules will be needed, taking into account high debt alongside the diversity of national positions. Yet, as Bilbiie et al. (2021) stress, proposals that might alleviate divergences, notably a system of cross-border transfers or genuine Eurobonds, continue to be resisted, largely because of a lack of political support for redistributive measures.

In an IMF paper, Arnold et al. (2022) sum up much of the recent debate on the reform of EU fiscal governance, observing that their proposals 'stand on the shoulders of several recent proposals but go further in seeking to strengthen implementation by Member States'. There is not, as table 2 in their paper demonstrates, a clear consensus on what needs to be done, although improving national 'ownership' so as to improve implementation and focussing more sharply on longer-term fiscal sustainability are prospective reforms supported by many contributors to the debate. Analysis in the European Commission (2022b) 2021 report on fiscal sustainability, noting the sizeable number of countries at risk and the threats to fiscal sustainability, confirms the implementation deficit.

What any fiscal stabilisation mechanism can realistically provide will depend on its scale, the mandate given to it and the terms on which it can be accessed, and the incentives for using it in preference to other means of dealing with an economic shock. Clearly, if an instrument has only a modest financial capacity, it will be incapable of acting to counter a 'symmetric' shock affecting all (or most) countries participating in the scheme, but may have value for an 'asymmetric' shock affecting only one or two participants. In practice, too, a modest scheme may be suitable for small countries, but ill-suited to larger ones.

Concerns about whether even the substantial credit line of the ESM would suffice to deal with one of the larger Eurozone members exemplify the last point. The 2015 package for Greece, an economy accounting for less than 2 per cent of Eurozone GDP, provided for loans of up to €86 billion, representing 17 per cent of the ESM's notional €500 billion capacity and close to 40 per cent of Greek GDP in 2015. Even if it is accepted that the Greek case is exceptional, the entire firepower of the ESM is equivalent to only about a quarter of the GDP of France or Italy. According to the ESM website, the Greek public finances in 2017 were better off by as much as 6.7 per cent of GDP because of the low interest rates payable on ESM loans.

The MacDougall (1977) report suggested a budget of 5–7 per cent of EU GDP; today it seems absurdly too high.[22] Clearly, defining the mandate for a new stabilisation instrument is tricky, not least because in the Eurozone context there is necessarily a cross-border dimension to any support: in emotive terms, one country's taxpayers would be called upon to fund another's. Net contributors to the system typically want to limit their risk of not being repaid and to insist on strict rules for accessing it. This translates, inter alia, into questions of the duration of the support, the terms on which it is offered and limits on the explicit or implicit fiscal transfer involved. Very favourable loan terms, for example, provide recipient governments with a net gain compared with prevailing market rates for the borrowing they would otherwise need.

Then there is how to limit the support to prevent it becoming a permanent system of transfers (a distributive aim that is not necessarily compatible with the stabilisation objective). The rationale for a stabilisation policy is to counter a temporary shock, but while this involves a fiscal transfer in the short term, it becomes something different if it endures. A true stabilisation instrument

---

[22] Even the hotly contested NGEU package falls far short of this level.

should work in both directions, including by transferring from poorer to richer participants if the conditions were met. Moreover, political economy considerations will loom larger if some countries are seen to be persistent takers while others only give.

7.4.1 Rules, Standards and Institutional Options

Despite broad agreement on the shortcomings of the EMU fiscal rules – especially the SGP – there is much less clarity on what should replace them and it remains to be seen whether the November 2022 proposals will garner support and go far enough. Blanchard et al. (2021) proposed a move away from numerical EU fiscal rules to what they call 'enforceable fiscal standards', instead of tweaking the parameters of existing fiscal rules. They maintain that the underlying macroeconomics of fiscal positions is 'a complex issue [in which] there is no single, time-country-invariant, magic debt or deficit number'.

A study carried out at the behest of Commissioner Gentiloni (High-Level Group on Post-Covid Economic and Social Challenges, 2022) argues for what it calls SGP 2.0 and NGEU 2.0. The former would exchange the word 'Stability' for 'Sustainability' in the Pact, with the objective of obliging governments to take account of future liabilities arising from dealing with climate change and social trends such as ageing. Regarding the latter, NGEU 2.0 would be a permanent fund aimed at investing in EU public goods, rather than a temporary transfer mechanism. The Group notes the need for democratic oversight and regards a strengthened role for the European Parliament as a key answer.

Complementary initiatives may be needed. They include the creation of a common safe asset (but probably falling short of fully fledged Eurobonds) establishing a Eurozone Treasury and the evolution of the Eurogroup president towards being a de facto finance minister. Some form of safe asset ought to be realisable, but a Treasury and a finance minister would be more sensitive. A common Treasury has been, in one form or another, under consideration since the earliest steps towards monetary integration. There has been some discussion about recasting the ESM and broadening its mandate, for example by enabling it to function as backstop for bank resolution. A true Treasury would, however, do much more. But when the functions of Treasuries elsewhere are examined, such as being responsible for issuing debt, heavy steering of national fiscal policy or even implementing 'federal' tax and spend policies, the political obstacles rapidly mount. Similar objections arise about proposals for a European-level minister of finance, perhaps modelled on the High Representative for External Affairs.

7.4.2 The Likely Influence of the Pandemic and the Ukraine War

The disruption from Covid-19 may prove to be both the greatest of tests for EMU but also the start of a new and potentially very different chapter. Having elicited rapid reactions by policymakers across Europe, in contrast to previous experience, actions at the EU or Eurozone level were quickly decided. New instruments were rapidly put in place, including a temporary unemployment insurance scheme – SURE – as well as the NGEU package aimed at bolstering the recovery. The ramifications of the Russian invasion of Ukraine and the sudden – and largely unanticipated – surge in inflation in 2022 pose further, but arguably similar, challenges.

In economic terms (as opposed to health considerations) Covid-19 had three, interrelated types of effects, visible to varying degrees in all EU countries. Lockdowns in whatever form, first, translated into a sudden, negative step-change in GDP, and increased public and private indebtedness. Second, there were uneven effects on different segments of the economy, whether by sector of activity or by locality. Tourism, transport services and regions most dependent on them were hit and recovery is far from complete in several countries. A key unknown will be whether the pre-virus structure of the economy will be largely restored as conditions normalise, or whether permanent shifts will occur.

Third, despite shielding policies from governments, households initially endured declines in disposable income and some job losses. These losses, only partly recovered by rapid growth in 2022, are again at risk from the surge in energy prices, partly as a consequence of the invasion of Ukraine. There is not only a return of inflation but also a movement of the terms of trade against EU countries in favour of Russia and other energy producers. The resulting stagflation may well abate relatively rapidly (in contrast to the late 1970s), but could accentuate divergence in the EU.

Two main consequences loom for the longer term. The first can be thought of as 'macro-prudential': as a result of the substantial increases in public debt to GDP ratios, arising from the combination of the decline in the denominator and the (entirely justified) exceptional spending envisaged. These debts will have to be serviced and, eventually, repaid or refinanced by governments burdened with much more fragile public finances, creating solvency risks. Likely knock-on effects for financial intermediaries could see a further manifestation of the 'doom-loop' identified a decade ago, especially if the pressures on some sectors aggravate non-performing loans.

Second, a 'scarring' effect of inactivity both on workers and on companies is a cause for concern. It can be countered by a mix of active labour market policies, a well-judged regulatory framework, support from employment agencies and appropriate incentives for workers. But in the present context, a more troubling scenario would be if the scarring extends to many employers because their detachment from their markets for what could be a lengthy period has a similar effect in eroding their ability to compete.

Governments are, and will remain, under unrelenting pressure to cushion the rise in the costs of living resulting from these developments. As Blanchard and Pisani-Ferry (2022) point out, the first-round effects are the inflation induced by the likely accentuation of the surge on energy prices from Russian restrictions on gas supply, and increased public spending associated with dealing with the flow of refugees and direct fiscal and military support for Ukraine. Longer term, the demands of an accelerated energy transition and commitments to increase defence spending will add to the strains on public finances.

All of this poses profound challenges for economic governance in Europe. Is debt to be avoided, tolerated or even encouraged? Is so much public spending going further to stoke up inflation, as standard economic theory might predict? What role can fiscal and other rules play in a world in which the parameters previously applied for many rules are so far from today's reality or enforcement is politically impossible?

8 Conclusions

'Many would be saddened by the death of the euro. But it's not the end of the world. Currencies come and go.'

– Joe Stiglitz, interviewed by *Time Magazine*[23]

As EU economic governance has been severely challenged in the last decade and, at times, found decidedly wanting, procrastination, indecision, kicking-the-can-down-the-road, lowest common denominator, fudge and out-of-touch elites are all watchwords not unreasonably applicable to it. Although the death-knell of the euro has been sounded many times, rumours of its demise – to misquote Mark Twain – continue to be more than exaggerated in the sense that the probability of it collapsing any time soon looks to be slender.

The more subtle question is whether the euro *ought* to survive in roughly its present form. The radical alternative is for it to break up because (as Stiglitz, 2016, implies in the title of his polemical and hard-hitting book) the 'common currency threatens the future of Europe' and will not easily be salvaged. He finds that 'there has been some progress in creating eurozone institutions since the euro crisis broke out, but not enough to make a single-currency system

---

[23] http://time.com/4457109/joseph-stiglitz-interview/.

work'.[24] But any sober assessment would conclude that the costs of break-up would be horrific, especially if in a disorganised manner. As the eminent journalist Martin Wolf observed in the *Financial Times* on 27 January 2015[25]:

> Creating the eurozone is the second-worst monetary idea its members are ever likely to have. Breaking it up is the worst. Yet that is where pushing Greece into exit might lead. The right course is to recognise the case for debt relief, conditional on achievement of verifiable reforms. Politicians will reject the idea. Statesmen will seize upon it. We will soon know which of the two they are.

The EU is not, and (*pace* a few diehards) is no longer likely to become, a truly federal entity. Instead of being on a pathway towards a United States of Europe, its ambitions are to be, at most, a United Europe of States. This is no mere wordplay. The key to understanding the political economy is that national positions are central, even more so in the aftermath of the years of crisis. Two questions nevertheless arise. First, have the EU and its institutions, the Eurozone in its many guises and the Member States gravitated towards a coherent system of economic governance for what is, to recall one of Jacques Delors' favourite expressions, 'an unidentified political object'? Second, has the pandemic (and, now, Ukraine) shifted the ground, making a step-change in governance more likely?

One answer is that, faced that with a structure that was in danger of falling to pieces, probably with catastrophic consequences, Europe's leaders have achieved a great deal against a politically inauspicious backdrop. The euro has not collapsed and, even though the political mood is often sour, European integration as a project is still on track. In short, there are new and more solid foundations on which to build. There are mixed, even contradictory, conclusions to draw about EMU's capacity to cope with crises. As proponents of the 'failing forward' view argue, there is a propensity to look for short-term solutions, yet to neglect longer-term reforms – a variation on muddling through – characterised by an inability to make the bolder institutional changes needed for stability.

Yet, as Jones et al. (2021, p. 1519) observe in assessing recent responses to crises: '[T]ime and again during the pandemic, the European Union appeared to fumble, only to pull itself together to forge a common response; time and again, that European response has turned out to be more effective than critics might have imagined and yet less than proponents might have wished.' Early indications from the response to the invasion of Ukraine suggest a similar verdict.

The unappealing answer is that the years of forced and often unsatisfactory compromises, despite repeated assertion of national interests, may have

---

[24] www.vanityfair.com/news/2016/08/a-nobel-winning-economist-has-a-plan-to-save-europe.
[25] www.ft.com/content/44c56806-a556-11e4-ad35-00144feab7de.

staunched the wounds but have put in place an edifice that will again prove vulnerable when tested in new and unforeseen ways. The slow progress in areas other than banking union and the time (and agonising) it took to arrive at a convincing and enduring solution for Greece testify to the depth of the challenges and the political obstacles. It may be best to acknowledge that this is simply how the EU works. Yet it can, on occasion, make great leaps. For example, the creation of the European Financial Stability Facility and the smaller European Financial Stabilisation Mechanism in 2010 and their use to finance the first Greek bailout happened over a weekend, admittedly with the leaders staring down the barrel of a gun – from the wrong end. Similarly, the marathon July 2020 European Council, culminating in the agreement of the NGEU, illustrates a willingness to countenance the previously unthinkable.

Difficult decisions and careful policy management will certainly be needed following the pandemic, while the Ukraine invasion poses new challenges. Economic trajectories are likely to be unbalanced as between Member States and sectors, potentially aggravating tensions. The EU collectively will have to find resources to respond to the various consequences of the war in Ukraine, at the same time as ramping up investment in countering climate change and digitalisation. As the Federal Reserve found after the global financial crisis, 'tapering' of the vast amounts of quantitative easing is problematic and it will be difficult to normalise – if at all possible – monetary policy. The large increase everywhere in public debt means that any rise in interest rates could lead to financing problems.

The compromises made in establishing EMU thirty years ago may have been unavoidable to enable it to proceed, but to arrive at a genuine or complete, and resilient, EMU, hard choices must be made. Otmar Issing put it succinctly in his response to the survey:

> EMU has reached a point at which a fundamental decision must be taken: should EMU be deepened/expanded into a fully-fledged fiscal and finally political union? If the answer is yes a fully transparent process of a change of the Treaty must be started. I am convinced it would be dangerous to hide political ambitions via democratically not legitimized actions of de facto transfer of national fiscal sovereignty to the European level.

8.1 Fiscal Reform

An irony about completing EMU is that there is plenty of agreement on what needs to be done. For economists, to a considerable extent, what is needed is an overhaul aimed at bringing the currency area closer to the optimality conditions so extensively analysed in six decades of scholarly literature on monetary integration. Yet, according to Thomas Wieser, there are still unanswered questions, especially, including whether there is a debt sustainability problem and, if so, whether a return to fiscal rules (whether or not reformed) is called for, and how to achieve any debt reduction (Wieser, 2021). For Thygesen et al. (2020), three imperatives are a genuine EU-level fiscal capacity, correcting the adverse incentives that deter growth-promoting public investment and a fiscal framework better attuned to national circumstances. Vitor Gaspar, who has been closely involved in the evolution of the euro from many perspectives during his distinguished career, put the challenge succinctly in a speech to a DG Ecfin workshop on fiscal rules: 'Creating a central fiscal capacity is one of the three critical unfinished jobs to complete the euro area architecture, along with completing the banking union and capital markets union.'[26]

In an interview with *Le Monde*,[27] Christine Lagarde appeared to advocate a permanent EU borrowing facility. Yet turning it into something permanent will be a politically demanding exercise, likely to provoke judicial challenges by interests hostile to sharing the burden. In part, the prospects depend on how well the NGEU is used, and any actual or perceived failings in this regard will foment opposition. Bilbiie et al. (2021) observe that 'it is easy to imagine a backlash against, and not more support for, any form of centralized fiscal policy and increased mutual insurance'. In this, and other areas, Treaty change – never an easy process – will probably prove necessary. Further taboos will clearly have to be broken, especially around risk-sharing, while reforms already in place need to be consolidated. For example, noting how progress on some of the elements of banking union has been stalled since the arrival of Covid-19, Anna Gelpern and Nicolas Véron argue for more rapid action to enhance bank resolution, observing that 'the bank crisis management framework remains a halfway house'.[28]

Coping with divergence in economic performance will be a further source of tension. Institutional developments have increased the differentiation between participating and non-participating Member States, with the latter neither incurring potential liabilities nor being afforded insurance against economic shocks (Schimmelfennig and Winzen, 2020). This is not a recipe for harmony.

---

[26] Workshop on 'Fiscal Rules in Europe: Design and Enforcement', DG ECFIN, Brussels, 28.01.2020, www.imf.org/en/News/Articles/2020/01/28/sp012820-vitor-gaspar-fiscal-rules-in-europe.

[27] Christine Lagarde: 'The new restrictions weigh on the recovery', *Le Monde* (19 October 2020), http://bit.ly/3gP7W8M.

[28] Anna Gelpern and Nicholas Véron, 'European banking reform should embrace a unitary approach to failed banks', Peterson Institute for International Economics (PIIE) (2 November 2020), http://bit.ly/3ERfKyX.

8.2 Legitimation and Leadership

Political and legal scholars see legitimation as the key and it will not be enough just to pay lip service to it. European integration can only properly be understood as a political project and is not easy to reduce to the kind of cost–benefit calculus that lies behind the rhetorical question: 'Are we better in or out?'. It follows that the euro and its governance, similarly, have to be assessed in terms of how they are interpreted and projected in Europe's political systems. Like it or not, procrastination and apparently contrary policies may make eminent sense in their political context. This is not to deny that egregious errors have been committed and that avoidable damage has been inflicted. There are, moreover, reasons to be sceptical about the European Parliament's ability to provide a bridge between 'normal' politics and decision-making at the EU level because, in Habermas' felicitous phrase,[29] 'this bridge is almost devoid of traffic'.

But no explanation can be forthcoming unless the highly contested nature of some of the decisions is brought into the equation. Given that fiscal promises tend to be at the heart of election campaigns, rules remove a core element of politics, leading the likes of Wyplosz (2012) to emphasise how much more difficult it is to legitimate fiscal rules (especially imposed or instigated by the supranational level) compared with assigning independence to monetary policy. In short, how the euro functions cannot be viewed largely through the prism of technocratic choices because of the many distributive ramifications of macroeconomic policy decisions. Governance has to embrace accountability mechanisms and ensure that different voices are heard. Vivien Schmidt (2020, p. 294) explains the many dimensions of legitimacy the EU/Eurozone has to confront.

> [It] has to come to grips with the realities of Member States' divided preferences, in particular between North and South; the institutional constraints imposed by the unanimity rule on treaties; the split-level legitimacy where output policies and throughput processes are generated at the EU level and input at the national; and the triple politicization of the EU—with increasing political contestation at the bottom, from the bottom up, and at the top.

If, then, what has to be done to arrive at a genuine EMU is so well understood, the obvious question is why is it not happening? Three answers emerge. First, Europe's leaders have struggled to agree on the sequencing of reforms. Lack of trust is a second answer, manifesting itself in many forms and frequently associated with the term 'moral hazard', but often also reflecting entrenched ideological differences. As Olivier Marty notes, '*la zone euro a essentiellement*

---

[29] Lecture on 'Democracy, solidarity and the European crisis' at the University of Leuven, 26.04.2012, http://bit.ly/3VvT2D8.

besoin d'une confiance affermie entre ses members [the Eurozone essentially needs greater trust among its members].[30] The third, more fundamental explanation is the continuing ambiguity about whether further economic integration is what is wanted.

In short, EMU has evolved considerably, but is still incomplete and will have to overcome a variety of obstacles if it is to be worthy of the adjective 'genuine'. The title of a paper by Wyplosz (2022b) sums up pithily where we are: 'The euro is fragile; that's OK.' He concludes that the threat of the euro collapsing, while not nil, is 'very, very low'. Solutions to technical problems of how to run the euro, though often difficult to agree and implement, can be found, but a complete and genuine EMU requires more. Mistrust among participating states has to be allayed; legitimacy has to be enhanced by offering citizens more convincing means of holding decision-makers to account; and better articulated approaches to solidarity and common interest are needed. Moreover, as Olivier Marty comments in his response to the survey, 'I do not think the fundamental determinants of reform have changed despite the crisis. ... Leaders are not up to the challenge collectively.'

Many of the metaphors around the crises affecting the euro have referred to politicians looking over the edge of the cliff and persuading themselves of the merits of not jumping. But retreat is not always the best answer. The leap now required is one over, instead of into, the abyss: political courage is needed to make the transition to a more complete, genuine EMU. Crisis management has reopened questions about who leads the Eurozone (Puetter, 2021), but a conclusion from this Element is that definitive answers remain elusive. Can Europe's leaders rise to these challenges?

---

[30] 'Réformes de la zone euro: doit mieux faire!', Revue Banque (1 Ocober 2019), http://bit.ly/3XJcGxo.

Appendix
List of Respondents to the Survey

Cinzia Alcidi, CEPS Brussels
Joaquin Almunia, former EU Commissioner for Economic and Financial Affairs
Laszlo Andor, FEPS-Europe
Piotr Arak, Polish Economic Institute
Bart van Ark, University of Manchester
Bertrand Badré, Blue like an Orange Capital
Roel Beetsma, University of Amsterdam and European Fiscal Board
Marek Belka, Former President of National Bank of Poland
Agnès Bénassy, Direction Générale du Trésor
Pervenche Berès, former chair of ECON Committee, European Parliament
Lorenzo Bini Smaghi, Chairman Société Générale
Massimo Bordignon, Universita Cattolica Milan and European Fiscal Board
Karlis Bukovskis, LIIA Riga
Marco Buti, European Commission
Hrvoje Butkovic, IMRO Zagreb
Nadia Calviño, Spanish Government
David Cameron, Yale University
Nauro Campos, University College London
Michele Chang, College d'Europe Bruges
Nicos Christodoulakis, Athens University of Economics and Business
Lorenzo Codogno, LCA Associates London
Jagjit Chadha, NIESR
Benjamin J. Cohen, University of California, Santa Barbara
Howard Davies, Chairman Natwest Bank
Zsolt Darvas, Bruegel Brussels
Anne-Laure Delatte, Université Paris Dauphine
Panicos Demetriades, University of Leicester
Paul De Grauwe, LSE
Jakob de Haan, Groningen University and De Nederlandsche Bank
Barry Eichengreen, University of California Berkeley
Michael Emerson, CEPS Brussels
Kevin Featherstone, LSE
John Fitzgerald, Trinity College and ESRI Dublin
Clemens Fuest, IFO Munich

Vitor Gaspar, IMF

Ernest Gnan, SUERF and Austrian National Bank

Daniel Gros, CEPS Brussels

Jérôme Haegeli, Swiss Re

Peter Hall, Harvard University

Randall Henning, American University

David Howarth, University of Luxembourg

Robert Holzmann, Governor of Austrian National Bank

Jacques Le Cacheux, Université de Pau et des Pays de l'Adour

Otmar Issing, Centre for Financial Studies, Frankfurt

Erik Jones, EUI Fiesole

Lars Jonung, former chair, Swedish Fiscal Policy Council

Sahoko Kaji, Keio University Tokyo

Bert Kuby, Committee of the Regions Brussels

Danae Kyriakopoulou, OMFIF

Michael Landesmann, WIIW Vienna

Martin Larch, European Commission

John Llewellyn, Llewellyn Consulting London

Sam Lowe, CER London

Alex Lucas Cole, Ufficio Parlamentare di Bilancio Rome

Corrado Macchiarelli, NESR

Nick MacPherson, House of Lords

Imelda Maher, University College Dublin

Michala Marcussen, Société Générale

David Marsh, OMFIF

Angelo Martelli, LSE

Olivier Marty, Science-Po

Niku Mättäänen, Helsinki University

Katherine McNamara, Georgetown University

Stefano Micossi, Assonime Rome

Reza Moghadam, Morgan Stanley

Erik Nielsen, Unicredit

Pier Carlo Padoan, former Italian Finance Minister

George Pagoulatos, Athens University of Economics and Business

George Papaconstantinou, EUI Fiesole

John Peet, *The Economist*

Jean Pisani Ferry, Science Po and EUI

Jonathan Portes, Kings College London

Vicky Pryce, CEBR London

Uwe Puetter, Flensburg University

Sonja Puntscher-Riekmann, Salzburg University

Klaus Regling, ESM

Olli Rehn, Governor of National Bank of Finland

Debora Revoltella, EIB

Martin Sandbu, *Financial Times*

Waltraud Schelkle, LSE

Holger Schmieding, Berenberg Bank

Ludger Schuknecht, formerly OECD

Robert Skidelsky, University of Warwick and House of Lords

David Smith, *The Sunday Times*

Mathieu Solal, freelance journalist

Rolf Strauch, ESM

Marjan Svetlicic, Ljubljana University

Sabine Syfuss-Arnaud, *Challenges*

Vivien Schmidt, Boston University

Ludger Schuknecht, formerly OECD

John Springford, CER London

György Szapáry, Hungarian National Bank

Poul Thomsen, Visiting Professor, LSE, former Director for Europe, IMF

Niels Thygesen, European Fiscal Board and University of Copenhagen

Raymond Torres, Funcas Madrid

Panos Tsakoglou, Greek Government

Loukas Tsoukalis, ELIAMEP Athens

Frank Vandenbroucke, University of Amsterdam and Belgian Government

Amy Verdun, University of Victoria Vancouver

Nicolas Veron, Peterson Institute of International Economics

Ramunas Vilpisauskas, Vilnius University

François Villeroy de Galhau, Gouverneur of La Banque de France

Boris Vujcic, Governor of Croatian National Bank

Paul Wallace, ex-The Economist

Marin Weale, Kings College London

Jakob von Weiszacker, BMF Berlin

Thomas Westphal, BMF Berlin

Thomas Wieser, Ex Eurogroup Working Group Chair

Peter Wostner, OECD

Charles Wyplosz, Graduate Institute, Geneva

References

Acocella, N. (2020) *The European Monetary Union: Europe at the Crossroads*, Cambridge: Cambridge University Press.

Aizenmann, J. (2016) 'Optimal currency area: A 20th century idea for the 21st century?', National Bureau of Economic Research (NBER) Working Paper No. 22097.

Alesina, A., Favero, C. and Giavazzi, F. (2019) *Austerity: When It Works and When It Doesn't*, Princeton, NJ: Princeton University Press.

Amtenbrink, F. (1999) *The Democratic Accountability of Central Banks: A Comparative Study of the European Central Bank*, Oxford: Hart.

Angeloni, I. (2020) *Beyond the Pandemic: Reviving Europe's Banking Union*, London: Centre for Economic Policy Research (CEPR), https://voxeu.org/content/beyond-pandemic-reviving-europe-s-banking-union.

Ardy, B., Begg, I., Hodson, D., Maher, I. and Mayes, D. G. (2006) *Adjusting to EMU*, Basingstoke: Palgrave.

Arnold, N., Balakrishnan, R., Barkbu, B. et al. (2022) 'Reforming the EU fiscal framework: Strengthening the fiscal rules and institutions', International Monetary Fund (IMF) Discussion Paper DP/2022/014, Washington, DC: IMF.

Baldwin, R. and Giavazzi, F. eds. (2015) *The Eurozone Crisis: A Consensus View of the Causes and a Few Possible Solutions*, Centre for Economic Policy Research (CEPR) e-book, http://voxeu.org/content/eurozone-crisis-consensus-view-causes-and-few-possible-solutions.

Bastian, J., Begg, I. and Fritz-Vannahme, J. (2011) *Making the European Union Work: Issues for Economic Governance Reform*, Gütersloh: Bertelsmann Stiftung.

Bayoumi, T., Eichengreen, B. and von Hagen, J. (1997), 'European monetary unification: Implications of research for policy, implications of policy for research', *Open Economies Review*, **8**, 71–91.

Begg, I. (2009) 'Regulation and supervision of financial intermediaries in the EU: The aftermath of the financial crisis', *Journal of Common Market Studies*, **47**(5), 1107–28.

Begg, I. (2014) 'Fiscal policy transparency', in Forssbaeck, J. and Oxelheim, L. eds., *The Oxford Handbook of Economic and Institutional Transparency*, Oxford: Oxford University Press, pp. 98–115.

Begg, I., Benedetto, G., Belicka, D. et al. (2022) *The Next Revision of the Financial Regulation and the EU Budget Galaxy*, Report to the European

Parliament, www.europarl.europa.eu/RegData/etudes/STUD/2022/721500/ IPOL_STU(2022)721500_EN.pdf.

Belke, A. and Klose, J. (2013) 'Does the ECB rely on a Taylor rule during the financial crisis? Comparing ex-post and real time data with real time forecasts', *Economic Analysis and Policy*, **41**(2), 147–71.

Bénassy-Quéré, A., Brunnermeier, M. K., Enderlein, H. et al. (2018) 'Reconciling risk sharing with market discipline: A constructive approach to euro area reform', Centre for Economic Policy Research (CEPR) Policy Insight No. 91, London: CEPR.

Bernanke, B. (2015) *The Courage to Act: A Memoir of a Crisis and Its Aftermath*, New York: W.W. Norton.

Bickerton, C. J., Hodson, D. and Puetter, U. (2015) *The New Intergovernmentalism: States and Supranational Actors in the Post-Maastricht Era*, Oxford: Oxford University Press.

Bilbiie, F., Monacelli, T. and Perotti, R. (2021) 'Fiscal policy in Europe: Controversies over rules, mutual insurance, and centralization', *Journal of Economic Perspectives*, **35**(2), 77–100.

Blanchard, O., Leandro, A. and Zettelmeyer, J. (2021) 'Redesigning EU fiscal rules: From rules to standards', Working Paper 21–1, Washington, DC: Peterson Institute for International Economics (PIIE).

Blanchard, O. and Pisani-Ferry, J. (2022) 'Fiscal support and monetary vigilance: Economic policy implications of the Russia-Ukraine war for the European Union', *Bruegel Policy Contribution* 06/2022, Brussels: Bruegel.

Blanchard, O., Sapir, A. and Zettelmeyer, J. (2022) 'The European Commission's fiscal rules proposal: A bold plan, with flaws that can be fixed', *Peterson Institute for International Economics* blog, https://www.piie.com/blogs/real time-economics/european-commissions-fiscal-rules-proposal-bold-plan-flaws-can-be-fixed

Blinder, A., Jordan, T. J., Kohn, D. and Mishkin, F. (2013) *Exit Strategy*, Geneva Report on the World Economy 15, London: Centre for Economic Policy Research (CEPR).

Bordo, M. D., Markiewicz, A. and Jonung, L. (2011) 'A fiscal union for the euro: Some lessons from history', National Bureau for Economic Research (NBER) Working Paper No. 17380, www.nber.org/papers/w17380.

Brunnermeier, M. K., James, H. and Landau, J.-P. (2016) *The Euro and the Battle of Ideas*, Princeton, NJ: Princeton University Press.

Buti, M. (2020) 'Enhancing Europe's economic global power', *Global Policy*, **11**(1), 147–50.

Buti, M., Giudice, G. and Leandro, J. (2018) 'Deepening EMU requires a coherent and well-sequenced package', *Voxeu*, https://voxeu.org/article/deepening-emu-requires-coherent-and-well-sequenced-package.

Buti, M., Giudice, G. and Leandro, J. eds. (2020) *Strengthening the Institutional Architecture of the Economic and Monetary Union*, VoxEU.org book, London: Centre for Economic Policy Research (CEPR), https://voxeu.org/content/strengthening-institutional-architecture-economic-and-monetary-union.

Campos, N., De Grauwe, P. and Ji, Y. eds. (2018) *The Political Economy of Structural Reforms in Europe*, Oxford: Oxford University Press.

Cecchetti, S. and Schoenholtz, K. (2016) 'A primer on helicopter money', *Voxeu/CEPR*, https://cepr.org/voxeu/columns/primer-helicopter-money.

Chang, M. (2018) 'The creeping competences of the European Central Bank during the euro crisis', *Credit and Capital Markets*, **51**(1), 41–53.

Cohen, B. J. (1994) 'Beyond EMU: The problem of sustainability', in Eichengreen, B. and Frieden, J. eds., *The Political Economy of European Monetary Unification*, Boulder, CO: Westview, ch. 8.

Cohen, B. J. (2015) *Currency Power: Understanding Monetary Rivalry*, Princeton, NJ: Princeton University Press.

Cohen, B. J. (2018) *Currency Statecraft: Monetary Rivalry and Geopolitical Ambition*, Chicago, IL: Chicago University Press.

Darling, A. (2012) *Back from the Brink: 1,000 days at No.11*, London: Atlantic Books.

Darvas, Z. and Leandro, A. (2015) 'The limitations of policy coordination in the euro area under the European semester', Bruegel Policy Contribution 2015/19. Brussels: Bruegel.

Davoodi, H., Elger, P., Fotiou, A. et al. (2022) 'Fiscal councils dataset: The 2021 update', International Monetary Fund (IMF) Working Paper 22/11, Washington, DC: IMF.

De Grauwe, P. (2013) 'Design failures in the Eurozone: Can they be fixed?' LSE 'Europe in Question' Discussion Paper Series No. 57/2013.

De Grauwe, P. (2022) *Economics of Monetary Union*, 14th ed., Oxford: Oxford University Press.

De Larosière, J. [chairman], Balcerowicz, L., Issing, O. et al. (2009) *The High-Level Group on Financial Supervision in the EU: Report*, Brussels, 25.02.2009, https://ec.europa.eu/economy_finance/publications/pages/publication14527_en.pdf.

Delors, J. (1989) 'Report on economic and monetary union in the European Community', Brussels, 17.04.1989, http://aei.pitt.edu/1007/.

Demetriades, P. (2020) *Central Bank Independence and the Future of the Euro*, Newcastle-upon-Tyne: Agenda.

Deroose, S., Carnot, N., Pench, L. R. and Mourre, G. (2018) 'EU fiscal rules: Root causes of its complexity', *Voxeu*, https://cepr.org/voxeu/columns/eu-fiscal-rules-root-causes-its-complexity.

Dyson, K. and Featherstone, K. (1999) *The Road to Maastricht: Negotiating Economic and Monetary Union*, Oxford: Oxford University Press.

Efstathiou, K. and Wolff, G. B. (2018) 'Is the European semester effective and useful?', Bruegel Policy Contribution 2018/09. Brussels: Bruegel.

Eichengreen, B. (2011) *Exorbitant Privilege: The Rise and Fall of the Dollar*, Oxford: Oxford University Press.

Eichengreen, B. (2014) 'The Eurozone crisis: The theory of optimum currency areas bites back', Notenstein Academy White Paper Series, https://eml.berkeley.edu/~eichengr/Swiss%20Bank%20White%20Paper%20No%202%20Text-1.pdf.

Eichengreen, B. (2015) *Hall of Mirrors: The Great Depression, the Great Recession, and the Uses – and Misuses – of History*, Oxford: Oxford University Press.

European Commission (2012) 'A blueprint for a deep and genuine economic and monetary union launching a European debate', Commission Communication, COM(2012) 777 final, Brussels, 28.11.2012.

European Commission (2015a) 'Making the best use of the flexibility within the existing rules of the Stability and Growth Pact', COM (2015)12, Brussels, 13.01.2015.

European Commission (2015b) 'Proposal for a regulation of the European Parliament and of the Council amending Regulation (EU) 806/2014 in order to establish a European Deposit Insurance Scheme', COM(2015)586, Strasbourg, 24.11.2015.

European Commission (2016) 'Vade Mecum on the Stability and Growth Pact: 2016 Edition' *European Economy Institutional Paper 021*.

European Commission (2018a) 'Towards a stronger international role of the euro', COM(2018) 796, https://ec.europa.eu/info/sites/info/files/com-2018-796-communication_en.pdf.

European Commission (2018b) 'Vade Mecum on the Stability and Growth Pact', Institutional Paper 75, Brussels: European Commission.

European Commission (2019) 'Vade Mecum on the Stability and Growth Pact', Institutional Paper 101, Brussels: European Commission.

European Commission (2020) 'Economic governance review', COM(2020) 55, Brussels, 5.2.2020, https://ec.europa.eu/info/sites/default/files/economy-finance/com_2020_55_en.pdf.

European Commission (2022a) 'Communication on orientations for a reform of the EU economic governance framework' COM(2022) 583, Brussels, 11.09.2022 https://economy-finance.ec.europa.eu/system/files/2022-11/com_2022_583_1_en.pdf

European Commission (2022b) *Fiscal Sustainability Report 2021*, European Economy Institutional Paper 171, Luxembourg: Publications Office of the European Union.

European Council (2012a) 'Towards a genuine economic and monetary union: Report by President of the European Council, Herman van Rompuy', EUCO120/12, Brussels, 26 June 2012.

European Council (2012b) 'Towards a genuine economic and monetary union', Brussels, 5 December 2012.

European Fiscal Board (2020) *Annual Report 2020*, Brussels: European Commission, https://ec.europa.eu/info/sites/default/files/efb_annual_report_2020_en_0.pdf.

Fabbrini, F. (2016) *Economic Governance in Europe: Comparative Paradoxes and Constitutional Challenges*, Oxford: Oxford University Press.

Feld, L. P., Fuest, C., Haucap, J. et al. (2021) 'The monetary policy strategy of the European Central Bank: Review and recommendations', Kronberger Kreis-Studien No. 67, Berlin: Stiftung Marktwirtschaft.

Ferran, E. and Babis, V. S. G. (2015) 'The European single supervisory mechanism', *Journal of Corporate Law Studies*, 13(2), 255–85.

Fuest, C. and Peichl, A. (2012) 'European fiscal union: What is it? Does it work? And are there really "no alternatives"?', IZA Policy Paper, 39, Bonn: IZA.

Goodhart, C. A. E. (1980) *Money Information and Uncertainty*, Boston, MA: MIT Press.

Gorter, J., Jacobs, J. and de Haan, J. (2008) 'Taylor rules for the ECB using expectations data', *Scandinavian Journal of Economics*, 110(3), 473–88.

Hamilton, A. (1790) 'First report on the public credit', Communicated to the House of Representatives, 14 January 1790, Treasury Department, https://archive.schillerinstitute.com/economy/2015/hamilton-first_report_on_the_public_credit.pdf.

Heipertz, M. and Verdun, A. (2010) *Ruling Europe: The Politics of the Stability and Growth Pact*, Cambridge: Cambridge University Press.

High-Level Group on Post-Covid Economic and Social Challenges (2022) *A New Era for Europe: How the European Union Can Make the Most of Its Pandemic Recovery, Pursue Sustainable Growth and Promote Global Stability*, Luxembourg: Publications Office of the European Union.

Hodson, D. (2011) *Governing the Euro Area in Good Times and Bad*, Oxford: Oxford University Press.

Hodson, D. (2021) 'The institutions of economic and monetary union: From the euro crisis to Covid-19', in Hodson, D., Puetter, W., Saurugger, S. and Peterson. J. eds., *The Institutions of the European Union*, Oxford: Oxford University Press.

Howarth, D. and Schild, J. (2022) 'Torn between two lovers: German policy on economic and monetary union, the New Hanseatic League and Franco-German bilateralism', *German Politics*, **31**(2), 323–43.

Issing, O., Gaspar, V., Angeloni, I. and Tristani, O. (2001) *Monetary Policy in the Euro Area Strategy and Decision-Making at the European Central Bank*, Cambridge: Cambridge University Press.

Jabko, N. (2015) 'The elusive economic government and the forgotten fiscal union', in Matthijs, M. and Blyth, M. eds., *The Future of the Euro*, Oxford: Oxford University Press.

Jones, E., Kelemen, R. D. and Meunier, S. (2021) 'Failing forward? Crises and patterns of European integration', *Journal of European Public Policy*, **28**(10), 1519–36.

Jonung, L. and Drea, E. (2010) 'It can't happen, it's a bad idea, it won't last: U.S. economists on the EMU and the euro, 1989–2002', *Econ Journal Watch*, **7**(1), 4–52.

Kaji, S. (2020) 'Strength in contradiction: Europe as a living example for peaceful prosperity', *Global Policy*, **11**(1), 151–4.

Kenen, P. B. (1992) *EMU After Maastricht*, Washington, DC: Group of Thirty.

Koester, G. and Sondermann, D. (2018) 'A euro area macroeconomic stabilisation function: Assessing options in view of their redistribution and stabilisation properties', ECB Occasional Paper No. 216.

Krugman, P. (2012) 'Revenge of the optimum currency area', in Acemoglu, D., Parker J. and Woodford, M. eds., *NBER Macroeconomics Annual*, 27.

Lane, P. R. (2012) 'The European sovereign debt crisis', *Journal of Economic Perspectives*, **26**(3), 49–68.

Leiner-Killinger, N., Lopez-Perez, V., Steigert, R. and Vitali, G. (2007) 'Structural reforms in EMU and the role of monetary policy: A survey of the literature', ECB Occasional Paper No. 66.

MacDougall, G. D. A. (1977) *Report of the Study Group on the Role of Public Finance in European Integration*, Luxembourg: OOPEC.

Maduro, M., Martin, P., Piris, J.-C. et al. (2021) 'Revisiting the EU framework: Economic necessities and legal options', Centre for Economic Policy Research (CEPR) Policy Insight. No. 114, London: CEPR.

Marsh, D. (2016) *Europe's Deadlock: How the Euro Crisis Could Be Solved – And Why It Still Won't Happen*, New Haven, CT: Yale University Press.

Matthijs, M. and Blyth, M. (2015) 'Conclusion: The future of the euro – possible futures, risk and uncertainties', in Matthijs, M. and Blyth, M. eds., *The Future of the Euro*, Oxford: Oxford University Press.

McNamara, K. R. (1998) *The Currency of Ideas: Monetary Politics in the European Union*, Ithaca, NY: Cornell University Press.

Mundell, R. (1961) 'A theory of optimum currency areas', *American Economic Review*, **51**(4), 657–65.

Papaconstantinou, G. (2019) *Whatever It Takes: The Battle for Post-Crisis Europe*, Newcastle-upon-Tyne: Agenda.

Papademos, L. (2014) 'A better EMU blueprint', *International Economy*, Winter, 34–7.

Pench, L. R., Ciobanu, S., Zgala, M. and Manescu, C. B. (2019) 'Beyond fiscal rules: How domestic fiscal frameworks can contribute to sound fiscal policy', *Voxeu*, https://cepr.org/voxeu/columns/beyond-fiscal-rules-how-domestic-fiscal-frameworks-can-contribute-sound-fiscal-policy.

Pisani-Ferry, J. (2014) *The Euro Crisis and Its Aftermath*, Oxford: Oxford University Press.

Pisani-Ferry, J. (2018) 'Euro area reform: An anatomy of the debate', Centre for Economic Policy Research (CEPR) Policy Insight 95, London: CEPR.

Pisani-Ferry, J. (2020) 'European Union recovery funds: Strings attached, but not tied up in knots', Policy Contribution 2020/19, Brussels: Bruegel.

Pomfret, R. (2021) *The Road to Monetary Union*, Cambridge: Cambridge University Press.

Puetter, U. (2012) 'Europe's deliberative intergovernmentalism: The role of the Council and European Council in EU economic governance', *Journal of European Public Policy*, **19**(2), 161–78.

Puetter, U. (2021) 'Who leads the euro zone? From crisis management to future reform', *Journal of European Public Policy*, **28**(1), 880–5.

Rehn, O. (2020) *Walking the Highwire: Rebalancing the European Economy in Crisis*, Basingstoke: Palgrave Macmillan.

Savage, J. D. and Howarth, D. (2018) 'Enforcing the European semester: The politics of asymmetric information in the excessive deficit and macroeconomic imbalance procedures', *Journal of European Public Policy*, **25**(2), 212–30.

Schelkle, W. (2018) *The Political Economy of Monetary Solidarity: Understanding the Euro Experiment*, Oxford: Oxford University Press.

Schmidt, V. A. (2020) *Europe's Crisis of Legitimacy: Governing by Rules and Ruling by Numbers in the Eurozone*, Oxford: Oxford University Press.

Schmidt, V. A. (2021) 'Europe's (euro) crisis of legitimacy', in Wallace, H., Koutsiaras, N. and Pagoulatos. G. eds., *Europe's Transformations: Essays in Honour of Loukas Tsoukalis*, Oxford: Oxford University Press.

Schimmelfennig, F. (2015) 'Liberal intergovernmentalism and the euro area crisis', *Journal of European Public Policy*, **22**, 177–95.

Schimmelfennig, F. and Winzen, T. (2020) *Ever Looser Union? Differentiated European Integration*, Oxford: Oxford University Press.

Schoenmaker, D. (2013) 'An integrated financial framework for the banking union: Don't forget macro-prudential supervision', *European Economy Economic Papers* 492.

Schuknecht, L. (2014) 'The empire strikes back: Why Germany's exports and current account surpluses benefit other countries', *International Economy*, Fall, www.international-economy.com/TIE_F14_Schuknecht.pdf.

Sinn, H.-W. (2014) *The Euro Trap*, Oxford: Oxford University Press.

Snaith, H. (2014) 'Narratives of optimum currency area theory and Eurozone governance', *New Political Economy*, **19**(2), 183–200.

Stiglitz, J. (2016) *The EURO and Its Threat to the Future of Europe*, London: Penguin.

Thygesen, N., Beetsma, R., Bordignon, M. et al. (2020) 'Reforming the EU fiscal framework: Now is the time', *Voxeu*, https://voxeu.org/article/reforming-eu-fiscal-framework-now-time.

Tobin, J. (2001) 'Currency unions: Europe versus the United States', *Policy Options*, May, 31–3.

Tsoukalis, L. (2016) *In Defence of Europe: Can the European Project Be Saved?*, Oxford: Oxford University Press.

Verdun, A. (2019) 'The European Central Bank', *Oxford Research Encyclopaedia Politics*, Oxford: Oxford University Press, https://oxfordre.com/politics/view/10.1093/acrefore/9780190228637.001.0001/acrefore-9780190228637-e-254?print=pdf.

Wallace, P. (2016) *The Euro Experiment*, Cambridge: Cambridge University Press.

Weiler, J. (2013) 'In the face of crisis: Input legitimacy, output legitimacy and the political messianism of European integration', *Journal of European Integration*, **34**(7), 825–41.

Werner, P. (1970) 'Report to the Council and Commission on the realisation by stages of economic and monetary union in the Community', *Supplement to Bulletin 11–1970 of the European Communities*, https://ec.europa.eu/economy_finance/publications/pages/publication6142_en.pdf.

Wessels, W., Schramm, L. and Kunstein, T. (2022) *The European Council as a Crisis Manager: The EU's Fiscal Response to the COVID-19 Pandemic*, Baden-Baden: Nomos.

Wieser, T. (2021) 'The post-coronavirus fiscal policy questions Europe must answer', *Bruegel blog post*, www.bruegel.org/2021/02/the-post-coronavirus-fiscal-policy-questions-europe-must-answer/.

Wyplosz, C. (2012) 'Fiscal rules: Theoretical issues and historical experiences', National Bureau for Economic Research (NBER) Working Paper 17884, www.nber.org/system/files/working_papers/w17884/w17884.pdf.

Wyplosz, C. (2020) 'The Euro area after Covid-19', European Parliament Monetary Dialogue Papers, November, www.europarl.europa.eu/cmsdata/214969/01.WYPLOSZ_final.pdf.

Wyplosz, C. (2022a) 'Reform of the Stability and Growth Pact: The Commission's proposal could be a missed opportunity' *VOXEU Column*, 17/11/2022, https://cepr.org/voxeu/columns/reform-stability-and-growth-pact-commissions-proposal-could-be-missed-opportunity

Wyplosz, C. (2022b) 'The euro is fragile; that's OK', European Policy Analysis 13/2022, Stockholm: Swedish Institute for European Policy Studies.

Zaretsky, A. M. (1998) 'Yes, this EMU will fly, but will it stay aloft?', Federal Reserve Bank of St. Louis, *Regional Economist*, July, 1–6.

Cambridge Elements

Economics of European Integration

Nauro F. Campos

University College London

Nauro F. Campos is Professor of Economics at University College London and Research Professor at ETH-Zürich. His main fields of interest are political economy and European integration. He has previously taught at CERGE-EI (Prague), California (Fullerton), Newcastle, Brunel, Bonn, Paris 1 Sorbonne and Warwick. He was a visiting Fulbright Fellow at Johns Hopkins (Baltimore), a Robert McNamara Fellow at The World Bank, and a CBS Fellow at Oxford. He is currently a Research Fellow at IZA-Bonn, a Professorial Fellow at UNU-MERIT (Maastricht University), a member of the Scientific Advisory Board of the (Central) Bank of Finland, and a Senior Fellow of the ESRC Peer Review College. He was a visiting scholar at the University of Michigan, ETH, USC, Bonn, UCL, Stockholm, IMF, World Bank, and the European Commission. From 2009 to 2014, he was seconded as Senior Economic Advisor/SRF to the Chief Economist of the UK's Department for International Development. He received his Ph.D. from the University of Southern California (Los Angeles) in 1997, where he was lucky enough to learn about institutions from Jeff Nugent and Jim Robinson and (more than) happy to be Dick Easterlin's RA. He is the editor in chief of Comparative Economic Studies, the journal of the Association for Comparative Economic Studies.

About the Series

This Element series provides authoritative, up-to-date reviews of core topics and recent developments in the field with particular emphasis on structural, policy and political economy issues. State-of-the-art contributions explore topics such as labour mobility, the euro crisis, Brexit, immigration, inequality, international trade, unemployment, climate change policy, and more.

Cambridge Elements ≡

Economics of European Integration

Elements in the Series

The Road to Monetary Union
Richard Pomfret

Completing a Genuine Economic and Monetary Union
Iain Begg

A full series listing is available at www.cambridge.org/EEI